AF679461

MANAGING YOUR FINANCIAL EXPECTATIONS

A Simple Plan for Millennials & Generation X

BOOK 1: A Quick Start Guide

I don't regret the things I've done,
I regret the things I didn't do when I had the chance.

Anon

ISBN: 978-1-918-07795-7

Published by UK Book Publishing (ukbookpublishing.com)

The author may be reached at **mark@MYFE.guide**

DEDICATION

This book is dedicated to my kids who make their mother and me so happy and so proud.

IN HOPE

The MYFE series of books are FREE to download or view online.

However, if you find them helpful, I hope you will consider making a donation to **The Brain Tumour Charity**, which I have chosen to support. Every donation is important, no matter how small. Thank you so much.

THE BRAIN TUMOUR CHARITY

Please donate to this charity at JustGiving (bit.ly/3iZhCe3)
My family and I have known the terror of brain tumours. We were lucky; we lived through it and came out the other side. Many don't.

Brain tumours are the biggest cancer killer of children and people under 40. In terms of the numbers of life years lost, it is the most fatal of all cancers. There are over 100 different types of brain tumour, and the number of people diagnosed with brain tumours is growing by 2% every year.

More research is desperately needed. Please help make a difference by donating as much as you can afford. Every bit helps. Thank you.

6th Century BC

Do the difficult things while they are easy and do the great things while they are small. A journey of a thousand miles begins with a single step.

Laozi, Chinese philosopher

21st Century AD

If you're walking down the right path and you're willing to keep walking, eventually you'll make progress.

Barack Obama, American President

BOOK PROTOCOLS

DIP IN AND OUT

Managing Your Financial Expectations has been written in such a way as to allow you to dip in and out of those topics that interest you most – hence the detailed Table of Contents. If you are reading the book in a digital format you will also notice there are many clickable cross references, these will allow you to jump back and forwards within the text as you wish.

HYPERLINKS

Hyperlinks are peppered throughout this book. These links were active at the time of writing, but some may have subsequently been moved, taken down or are now hidden behind paywalls.

For those of you reading this book in hard copy, there is an abbreviated weblink where appropriate immediately after the blue hyperlink. For example, if you wanted to access this book online you can click MYFE.guide or you could type **bit.ly/3xrLXaJ** into your browser. I have deleted the 'https://' as this should be automatically inserted by your browser. Where there is no abbreviated link just type in the name.

I have included these links for their helpfulness, but I am in no way responsible for their content.

RECOMMENDATIONS

If you're wondering, I have never met, spoken to nor communicated with any of the owners/authors of the various websites/books/blogs/services I recommend throughout MYFE. They don't even know who I am – there are no kickbacks here! My decision to recommend them to you is based purely on my perception of the quality and practical value of their work.

YOUR HELP PLEASE

If you have any observations or suggestions to make, please email me at **mark@MYFE.guide**. I will be happy to include any additional topics or examples you might suggest in future editions. As well as offering your overall impression, it would be most appreciated if you mention which topic or section of the book you found most and least helpful. Writing this book has been a learning process for me too!

TESTIMONIALS

If you've found the book helpful, please be kind enough to email me a testimonial at **mark@MYFE.guide**. These will be used to give others who visit the website a sense of whether or not to invest their time in reading the book.

THE USE OF JARGON

Some of the terms used in this book will not be familiar to all readers. When such a term first appears a non-technical explanation will usually be given, sometimes in the sidenotes.

At the same time a link has been placed in the footer of every other page to give you quick access to any confusing investment jargon. This glossary by The Motley Fool is UK focused and well written.

DRM-FREE

This book doesn't use digital rights management (DRM) in any way because DRM makes life harder for everyone. May I therefore ask a favour: if a friend or contact wants a copy of the book, please direct them to the MYFE.guide website where they can download their own free copy, rather than emailing them your copy. Why do I ask this of you? Simply because by downloading their own copy they will be kept abreast of any corrections, updates, special articles and additional resources available. Thank you.

The MYFE.guide website does not accept any form of advertising, so neither you nor your family or friends will be pestered by emails from other organisations, and you will not receive promotions from third-party vendors.

DISCLAIMER

I am not a qualified financial adviser and do not provide personal investment advice.

I am not registered with the FCA.

The ideas, concepts and everything else in this book are simply my opinion based on what I've experienced over the years of my investment journey. It may not continue to work for me and it may not work for you in the future.

While I hope the book answers many of your questions and provides valuable guidance, I cannot possibly know the full details of any reader's personal situation, needs, investment goals or attitude to risk.

As the author, I make no representations as to accuracy, completeness, timeliness, suitability, or validity of any information in this book and will not be liable for any errors, misinterpretations, omissions or delays in this information or any losses, injuries or damages arising from its display or use.

Please conduct your own due diligence, or consult an FCA authorised financial adviser or broker before making any and all investment decisions. Any investments, trades, speculations, or decisions made on the basis of any information found in these books, expressed or implied, are undertaken at your own risk, financial or otherwise.

All information is provided on an as-is basis. You are solely responsible for your own choices. There are absolutely no guarantees.

WHY READ THIS BOOK?

There are two great reasons to read this book. 1) Most books on saving and investing are expensive and long – this book is free and short. 2) But the best reason to read this book is this: your future financial wellbeing depends on it.

Most of us are too busy living life, or just surviving it, to consider our financial futures, telling ourselves that financial planning can wait. That's a mistake. Time is your greatest ally in securing a better financial future. But freedom from financial worry requires a plan. This book, along with the other books in the Managing Your Financial Expectations (MYFE) series, will give you that plan.

You'll be amazed at how simple the plan is. And it will only take half-an-hour of your time once a year. That said, it is not a 'get-rich-quick' plan (they don't exist).

If you're a member of Generation X (born between 1965 and 1980) or a Millennial (born between 1981 and 1996) – this book is for you. You're probably working full-time, and in need of advice on saving and investing your money. As this book explains: time is of the essence. The sooner you start saving and investing, the healthier your finances will be when eventually you retire.

You may think you haven't got time to read this book, so let me put it to you this way: if you don't read about saving and investing now, you'll have plenty of time wishing you had over the 20 plus years you're expected to live in retirement.

If you perceive the prospect of saving and investing as intimidating or frankly boring, allow these books to prove you wrong on both counts. These books are short but comprehensive – they outline all the key information you need. I hope they inspire you to take the necessary actions today to achieve your financial goals.

Here are just some of the benefits of this first book:

- It quickly answers the most frequently asked questions about saving and investing.
- It offers advice and ideas for getting out of debt and how to start saving.
- It's simple, and yet reveals a plan which only takes 30 minutes of your time each year, but over time will help you outperform most professional investors.
- It gives you a heads-up about the financial and emotional hurdles you'll face and how to overcome them. Not only that, it will show you how to seize the opportunities that arise from them.
- It describes how to invest tax-efficiently so your money grows faster. Even if you won the lottery or inherited a bundle, you'll still need this advice.
- It discusses what you should do if you have a defined benefit or a defined contribution pension plan with your employer. And how much the government will give you, even if you don't have an employer or an income.
- It incorporates numerous hyperlinks and references should you wish to explore specific topics.
- It doesn't try to sell you anything. There is no agenda here, other than to give you concise and practical information.
- It tells you when you need the services of a financial planner/adviser, and how much it will cost.
- It explains why investment common sense is not that common.
- It gives you realistic growth rates to anticipate from your investments (I'm afraid they're probably lower than you expect).
- It identifies why some people are successful investors while others fail miserably.
- It's free at MYFE.guide. This website does not accept any form of advertising, nor sell any of your data.
- It has a special edition for those with dyslexia.

BUT FIRST...

I know only two secrets to more consistently achieving success: **Homework** and **Hardwork**.

These books are designed to make the homework easier for you. The next step, the hard work, is up to you. Whether you retire financially secure and content, or financially insecure with all the attendant anxieties that can bring, is up to you.

MONEY IS A RESOURCE. You need to learn how to earn it, save it, manage it, spend it and grow it.

HELP SPREAD THE KNOWLEDGE
If you think your family, friends or contacts might benefit from this free book please send them a link to the MYFE website by visiting MYFE.guide

HERE'S THE ISSUE

Figure 1 is based on data from the Office for National Statistics (ONS) and illustrates the current situation with regards to the UK's personal savings. Figure 2 gives the picture with respect to the nation's pensions. Add the two together and while some will have a secure and financially worry-free retirement, most won't.
The medium pension pot for someone approaching retirement is £91,200, which generates an annual income of £3,040.
A long way from ideal.

Most will be overly dependent on their state pension, currently £9,000.[1] And if you think owning your own home is the answer, please think again – it just isn't that simple (see page **59**).

The message is: your financial expectations are best served by starting your saving and investment journey ASAP. **That means saving as much as you can as soon as you can and doing it as tax efficiently as possible.**[2]

However, and despite what you may think, saving to meet your financial expectations is not quite the burden it at first appears.

Tax efficient wrappers, such as pensions and ISAs, together with government and employer pension top-ups turbo-charged by the magic of compounding will do much of the hard work for you. The key to success is to have a plan and implement it now.

Like many, I didn't wake up to the need to save and invest until my forties. It wasn't too late, but it would have made a significant difference (and been considerably less stressful) had I started earlier. And when I did finally start, I made some impressive blunders.

So I wrote a memo to my kids to help them avoid the same grief. That memo became this MYFE series of books.

Experience is a hard teacher: it gives the test first and the lesson afterwards. In writing these books I hope you will benefit from my experience and thus have the lessons before being faced with any painful tests. All the books in the MYFE series are designed to help you recognise and approach some of the financial choices with which you'll be confronted, as well as identify the positive options available to you.

1. Assuming you've made 35 years of National Insurance Contributions (NIC).

2. If you're uncomfortable committing to the regulatory constraints of a pension, invest through an ISA (see page **44**).

3. Occam Investing is a fabulous blog for those approaching, or already participating in, the investment markets. Clearly written with helpful graphics to reinforce common sense investment principles based on reliable and validated data. One of my favourite 'go-to' resources (see page **78**).

4. The self-employed are generally less inclined to invest in pensions, with roughly half having no pensions at all.

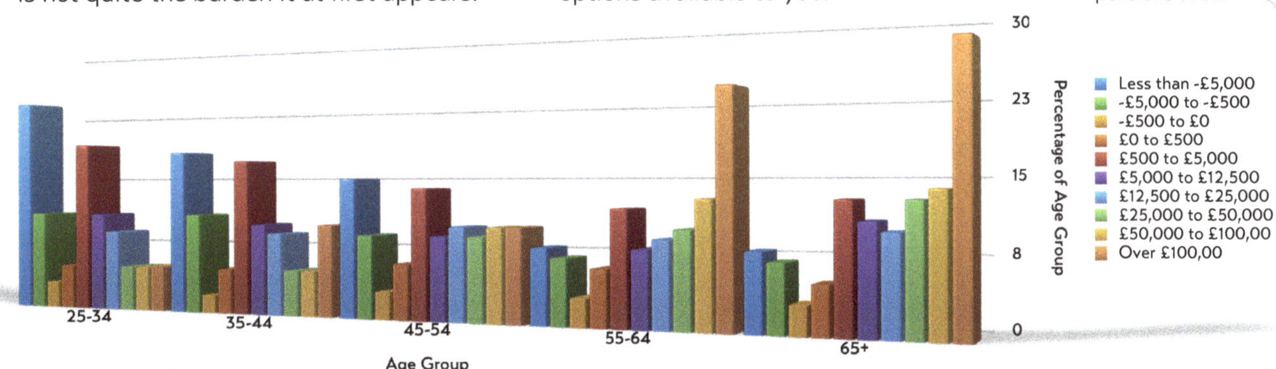

Figure 1. UK savings (including ISAs) by age as at November 2020 (excludes personal property and pensions)
Source: Occam Investing [3]

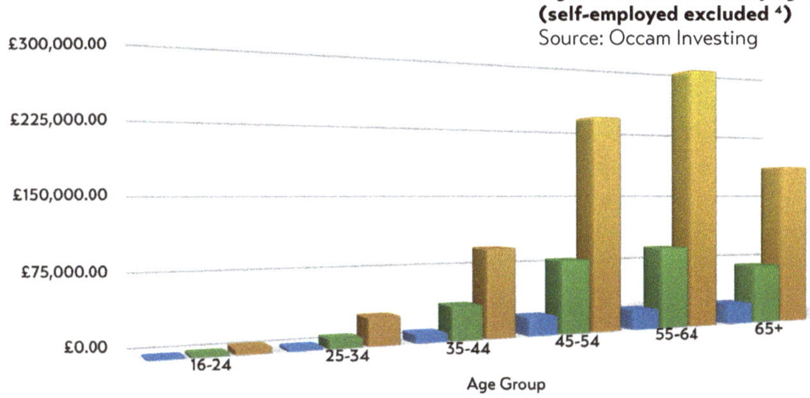

Figure 2. Pension size by age (self-employed excluded [4])
Source: Occam Investing

Interpreting percentiles in Figure 2: If, for example, you lined up everyone in the 55-64 age bracket in order of smallest pension savings to largest pension savings, the person who's 25% along the line has £21,600, the person right in the middle of the line has £91,200, and the person 75% along the line has £295,000.

OTHER BOOKS IN THE MYFE SERIES

Available as free downloads from MYFE.guide

If you've found this first book in the MYFE series helpful, you might want to consider books two and three. All books are written for the varying financial needs of Millennials and Generation X and are available in multiple formats.

In essence the narrative of the **MYFE** series of books trace the following structure:

- **MYFE Book 1: the What**
- **MYFE Book 2: the Why**
- **MYFE Book 3: the How**

BOOK 2: HOW INVESTMENT MARKETS PERFORM

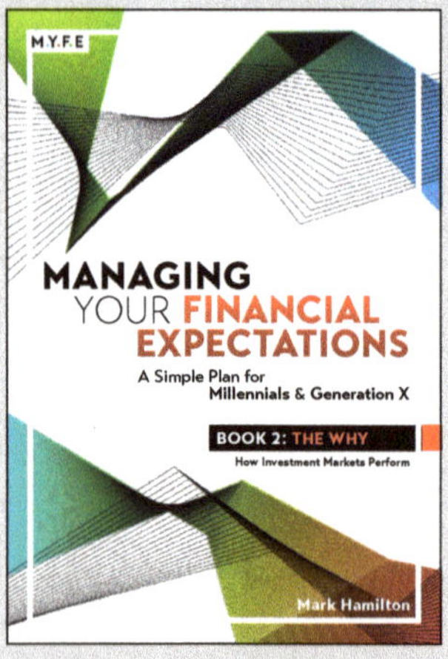

Book 2 is structured to give you a better understanding of how the investment markets, and the many asset classes within them, have delivered for investors over time. It tells you how to break through confusing market terminology, and focus on the returns which matter most to you. There are numerous infographics, so if you're short of time, just look at the pictures – they tell their own story. Additionally, this book arms you with vital questions to ask of any financial adviser before allowing them to manage your money. The ultimate purpose of Book 2 is to show you how the investment markets perform over time, and thus why you should consider acquiring the confidence to invest your savings in them.

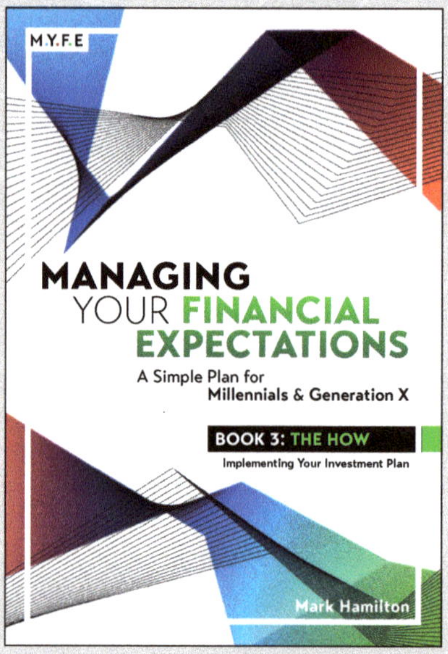

BOOK 3: IMPLEMENTING YOUR INVESTMENT PLAN

Too many investment guides tell you what to do, but not how to do it; they point you to the playground, but don't tell you which swings and roundabouts are most fun and safe, and which are dangerous. **MYFE Book 3** shows you valid alternatives for where (which platforms) and how (which funds) to invest your savings depending on your personal financial objectives (short, medium or long-term), and appetite for risk. Your partner should not use the same investment platform as you, as that increases your exposure to something called 'Operational Risk'. Book 3 therefore outlines alternative approaches for you and your partner, even if you're both the same age with the same financial goals/expectations. In short, Book 3 walks you through the online mechanics of investing. Once again, there are many infographics illustrating the multiple steps and choices available to you and/or your partner.

Still not sure? Then head over to MYFE.guide and read the sample page for the edition when it's published. Doing this will enable you to decide if either book warrants the investment of your time.

Glossary **of investment terms (bit.ly/3sCRxUO)**

Service to others is the rent you pay for your room here on Earth.

Muhammad Ali

INTRODUCTION

Most of us work to live, not live to work. That's because we need to earn money to survive. The irony is that the immediacy, excitement and pressures of today impede us from planning for tomorrow. And yet, in neglecting to consider our financial futures we're missing an incredible opportunity.

What's the point of working 40 plus years if at the end of all that hard graft, you're still having to worry if you've got enough to get by? Such an outcome leads only to a state pension, roughly £9,000 per annum or £175 per week. If all you have is £175 per week [5] to pay for absolutely everything, you already know that's not going to be enough.

Failing to plan for your financial welfare is planning for a life of insecurity and worry. Since we're expected to live at least 20 years in retirement, that's a long time to ponder and regret the steps you could have taken to be more financially secure.

With that in mind, this series of books on Managing Your Financial Expectations (MYFE) will help you develop an effective financial plan. It won't be easy, but then, little of true value is.

HELPING OTHERS

There are those of course who face great difficulty in helping themselves: the mentally and/or physically challenged. It is for them, as well as ourselves, that we should strive to achieve financial self-reliance. The less we personally need and take from the State, the more resources the State can direct – at least in theory – to those who genuinely need it.

Your first challenge is finding the motivation and time to read these books. Fear not. My initial task is to help you get started on your financial journey as quickly and sensibly as possible. To that end I have written this Quick Start Guide, which is not so much a book as a booklet. If you read nothing else, please read this. It's only a few pages and will inform your approach to managing your financial expectations.

PONTIFICATION ALERT!

I have spoken to many people while writing these books, and often heard the lament 'It's alright for some, they're lucky.' This is often true, but it's no reason for any of us to abandon hope of financial independence on the basis it's all down to luck. It isn't. The more responsibility we take for our own lives, the luckier we get.

If you watch and listen closely you will probably find those approaching financial wellbeing have consistently made numerous small, and sometimes painful, but ultimately rewarding, decisions regarding how they manage their money. They have learnt self-denial, discipline and patience, then applied these characteristics to their unique financial circumstances. It doesn't matter if those individuals come from tough backgrounds or privileged ones. People from all backgrounds have made a financial success of their lives.

On my personal financial path, I have tried to avoid fatalism by framing luck as something we are given, and fortune as what we choose to make of it. In other words, you can't choose the cards, but you can always play the hand you're dealt. That said, be mindful that creating good fortune from bad luck is not easy, and recognising opportunity from good luck can be challenging.

5. Assuming you've made 35 years of qualifying National Insurance Contributions.

WHY LEARN HOW TO INVEST?

Those who trust to chance must abide by the results of chance. They have no legitimate complaint against anyone but themselves.

Calvin Coolidge, American President

Recently I was taken aback by a seemingly innocuous comment on the radio. During an interview about investing one interviewee stated:

I don't want to be bothered to learn about investing, I just want a decent return for my money.

Really? That's one heck of a statement. The individual was not talking about using an investment adviser, but simply bemoaning the state of capitalism and the greed of others. Presumably the person who made this remark failed to recognise the inherent hypocrisy of their statement; he didn't want to be bothered to play his part in his own financial future, but expected others to make all the effort for him. If you expect others to do all the running you will pay for it, and will thus be unlikely to get a decent return. Furthermore, no one, absolutely no one, can be expected to care for your money as diligently as you.

If you strip the statement down, you're left with:

I don't want to be bothered... I just want...

Call me old fashioned, but I'm not persuaded most things in life work that way. If you get something without having made an effort to earn it, that's just luck. Successful investment strategies are not built on luck, but on informed choices.

An investment in knowledge pays the best interest.

Benjamin Franklin (1706 - 1790)

To make informed choices you're going to have to invest in yourself to become better informed. That's where this book comes in. As you work your way through it you may well become a bit confused. Don't worry, join the club!

As you 'learn' more, if your confidence doesn't go down before it goes up, then you probably aren't learning.

Jason Zweig, investment commentator and author of Your Money & Your Brain

Nothing of true value (except children) comes without at least some homework and hard work. Saving and investing are just the same.

As I've said, good or bad luck is what we're given, good or bad fortune is what we make of it. The difference is in our ability to make choices. Becoming financially independent requires making choices. As the champion golfer, Arnold Palmer, is reputed to have replied when asked why he was so lucky:

The harder I practice the luckier I get.

The point is: saving and investing for a more secure tomorrow will require some effort, beginning with acquiring the knowledge. Relying on others, while relieving you of effort, will cost you. The cumulative impact of compounding could – as you will learn – make these costs very high indeed.

TAKEAWAY

Intimidating though it may seem at first, one way or another you will have to learn the basics of saving and investing if you wish to reach your financial expectations.

Finally, learning about saving and investing requires setting personal goals and planning. Knowing how to set goals is an acquired skill. A goal without a plan is just a wish. There are many videos on YouTube and TED Talks covering the topic of setting and achieving goals. Here's one I like by Brian Tracy (**bit.ly/2JFLv4R**), it's packed with pearls of wisdom (but you'll have to practise them in earnest to really appreciate their value). It took me many years to learn the essence of what Brian conveys in seven minutes.

A GREAT STARTER BOOK

For those of you unfamiliar with financial terminology, and especially investment jargon, you might want to first consider reading Your Money Matters (bit.ly/33BGWzG). This is a free download published by Martin Lewis (the innovator of MoneySavingExpert.com). It is short, clearly written and beautifully illustrated. I recommend it.

PART **ONE**

Planning is bringing the future into the present so you can do something about it now.

Alan Lakein, author on personal time management

THE OVERALL PLAN

What would you think if someone told you there's an investment strategy anyone can understand, will only take half-an-hour of your time each year, will outperform 80% of finance professionals in the long run, and make you financially self-sufficient, possibly even well-to-do, in retirement?

Well, it's true, and here it is:

- Start by saving 15% – or as much as you can – of your monthly net income as soon as possible.
- Begin by paying off your debt and establishing an emergency fund of, say, three to six months' living expenses.[6]
- Once you've paid down your debt and have a realistic emergency fund, then you can begin to invest your savings. First make sure you place those savings into a tax wrapper, e.g. a pension or an ISA.
- Then select a platform and funds in which to invest your savings.[7]

That's it! Sounds simple doesn't it?

'Whoa!' I hear you say, 'If it's that simple, how come everyone doesn't do it, and how come we aren't all rich?' The answer is because while investing is simple to understand, it isn't easy to do.

Look at it this way: you will get trim and healthy if you exercise more and eat less. That's a simple plan. Dieting and investing plans are both simple, but neither dieting nor investing is easy. Joining a gym won't make you fit. You have to actually get on the treadmill. Investing is just like dieting and getting fit, you will face many temptations and distractions along the way. Your discipline and patience are therefore vital allies, and that means acknowledging the greatest barrier to meeting your financial expectations is **YOU**. Only you can decide how determined you are to save and invest for your future.

6. How much of an emergency fund you have is best established by estimating how long it will take you to find an alternative and regular job/income.

7. I recommend which specific platform(s) and fund(s) in **MYFE Book 3: Implementing Your Investment Plan.**

MAKE NO MISTAKE, achieving even your first two priorities will be hard; you will need to be focused. You can spend freely now while the future and your retirement seem light years away, or you can learn the skill of delayed gratification to make the necessary sacrifices, and increase your chances of a financially stress-free and happier retirement. Unless you win the lottery or inherit a substantial sum, you can't have it both ways. It's your call.

YOUR FIVE MAJOR HURDLES

The five major hurdles you will face during your saving and investment journey are as follows:

I love money. I love everything about it. I bought some pretty good stuff. Got me a $300 pair of socks. Got a fur sink. An electric dog polisher. A gasoline powered turtleneck sweater. And, of course, I bought some dumb stuff.

Steve Martin, actor, comedian, author and musician

1 **Learning to live within your means.** You cannot save, and cannot invest, if you do not spend less than you earn. You can either try to earn more or find ways to spend less, preferably both. The choice is yours: if you don't save, you'll die poor.

2 **Appreciating the basics of financial market history and the concept of investment risk.** The investment industry is keen to make financial markets appear complex and intimidating. They're not and it isn't.

3 **Understanding the mechanics of investing.** This is not the same as appreciating the basics of financial market history. Understanding the mechanics of investing requires a basic knowledge of the various investment options, tax advantages and investment structures currently available to you. Grasping these essential elements of successful investing is important, but it is not difficult.

4 **Avoiding the money grabbers.** Be warned: the investment community is full of charlatans – be they individuals or companies – whose aim is to transfer your wealth to themselves. You need to be able to recognise these hucksters and steer clear of their tricks and honey traps.

5 **Managing your own behaviour.** When it comes to investing, investment common sense is not that common. Once you begin your investment journey this will probably become your greatest challenge. The ups and downs of investment markets provoke many investors to panic. Giving in to these emotions causes instinctive, but counter-productive, behaviours.

LEARNING TO LIVE WITHIN YOUR MEANS

It's a big ask, but if you can save £20 a day on average, and invested that saving, it will be nominally worth £1,605,196 in forty years' time (based on 7% annual growth). If you manage £5 a day it will be worth £401,299 (see **Table 1** for more examples).

People spend too much. Social media and product advertising encourage us to spend, spend, spend. Why? Because, apparently, and according to L'Oréal, 'We're worth it!' We have come to think of the latest smartphone, Netflix subscription, gym membership, takeaways / frequent meals out, annual overseas holidays, expensive branded clothes, leasing new cars, and a latté whenever we feel like it as entitlements. They're not. These are all personal choices we make that can seriously damage our financial health.

Years	Save £5 daily		Save £10 daily		Save £15 daily		Save £20 daily	
	Saving p/m	Worth	Saving p/m	Worth	Saving p/m	Worth	Saving p/m	Worth
10	£152	**£26,462**	£304	**£52,925**	£456	£79,387	£608	**£105,849**
15	£152	**£48,459**	£304	**£96,919**	£456	£145,378	£608	**£193,837**
20	£152	**£79,643**	£304	**£159,285**	£456	£238,928	£608	**£318,571**
25	£152	**£123,849**	£304	**£247,698**	£456	£371,547	£608	**£495,397**
30	£152	**£186,517**	£304	**£373,035**	£456	£559,552	£608	**£746,069**
35	£152	**£275,357**	£304	**£550,714**	£456	£826,072	£608	**£1,101,429**
40	£152	**£401,299**	£304	**£804,598**	£456	£1,203,897	£608	**£1,605,196**
Total monthly deposits		£72,960		£145,920		£218,880		£291,840
Compounded returns		£328,339		£658,678		£985,017		£1,313,356
FINAL VALUE (after 40 years)		£401,299		£804,598		£1,203,897		£1,605,196

Table 1. Value of Daily Savings at 7% Compounded Nominal Returns [8]

At first glance the numbers in Table 1 appear amazing, if not unbelievable. Nevertheless, they're true. However, it's vital to understand two key components underpinning how these figures are derived:

- They are based on a consistent 7% annual return. You are unlikely to find an investment offering such high levels of consistent return over such a long period. As you may be aware, stock market returns are variable and volatile, and are not always positive.
- They are 'nominal' returns. Nominal returns are those calculated before inflation. Thus, while saving £20 daily for 40 years gives you a nominal return of £1,605,196, if inflation runs at a consistent 2% every year for 40 years, that £1,605,196 is only worth £726,978 in terms of actual purchasing power in year 40. Or, to express it another way, you would need £3,544,336 in 40 years' time to have the same purchasing power as £1,605,196 has today.

In other words, while the outcomes in Table 1 are accurate, they are unrealistic. Your rates of return and inflation have a huge impact on your eventual saving pot. There are no guarantees.

Nevertheless, and despite the difficulty of forecasting rates of return and inflation, the fundamental point holds good, namely: saving then investing are the most critical elements in your journey to financial security.

No one is expecting you to live a monastic existence, but it will help greatly if you learn to curb your impulse purchases and review your spending habits against what really matters to you. Two interesting articles from MyMoneyWizard on this subject can be found here (**bit.ly/2WGCk7g**) and here (**bit.ly/3bmOqYm**). MyMoneyWizard is a US blog, but don't let that put you off – the advice makes good sense wherever you live.

Beware of having small expenses; a small leak will sink a great ship.

Benjamin Franklin

Let's be frank, saving 15% of your salary is going to be tough – at least initially. If your after-tax earnings are £30,000 a year, that's £375 every month you've got to put aside. And, of course, before you can begin to save you'll have to get yourself out of debt first.

If you want to play around with your own assumptions about saving, here's (**bit.ly/32MxCZp**) a useful online calculator (see Figure 3).

BY THE WAY...

There are many books, blogs and YouTube videos on how to save money. Saving is all well and good, but the primary focus of your efforts should be how to EARN more money. By increasing your income you can save and invest more. There's a telling graph relating your savings rate to the time it will take you to reach financial independence here (**bit.ly/2LRSn0g**).

One way to increase your income is to develop a 'side hustle' (for some ideas see VitalDollar (**bit.ly/3baB9lw**) or BBC (**bbc.in/2xHl8F6**) and on page **80** in the Appendix. Perhaps the most realistic strategy for increasing your income is to invest your best efforts in your full-time job or primary role (assuming you enjoy it!).

I have worked with many skilful people, but it was always those most committed to their work and their company, rather than the most talented, who received the promotion and the extra income that came with it.

8. Figures have been compounded monthly on the assumption you transfer your daily savings into your investments at the beginning of each month. It is also assumed your investments are in a tax wrapper, such as an ISA or pension (see page **39**).

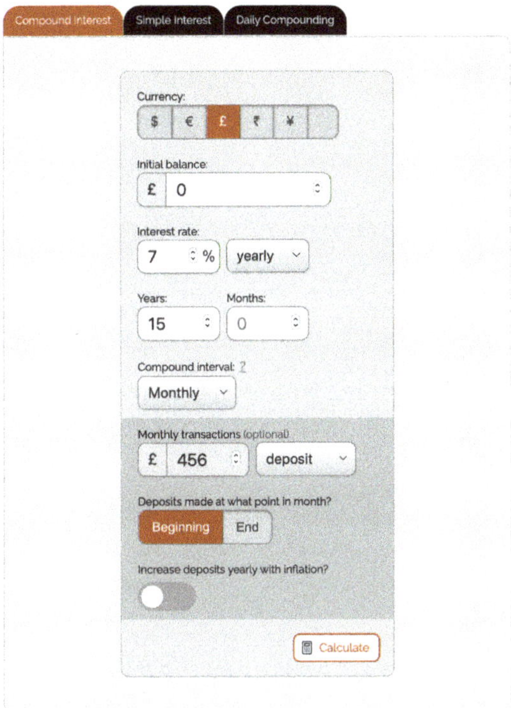

Final investment value
£145,377.93

Initial balance
£0.00

Total interest earned
£63,297.93

Total monthly deposits
£82,080.00

Effective Annual Rate (APY)
7.229%

Year	Year Deposits	Year Interest	Total Deposits	Total Interest	Balance
1	£5,472.00	£211.98	£5,472.00	£211.98	£5,683.98
2	£5,472.00	£622.88	£10,944.00	£834.86	£11,778.86
3	£5,472.00	£1,063.48	£16,416.00	£1,898.34	£18,314.34
4	£5,472.00	£1,535.93	£21,888.00	£3,434.27	£25,322.27
5	£5,472.00	£2,042.53	£27,360.00	£5,476.80	£32,836.80
6	£5,472.00	£2,585.76	£32,832.00	£8,062.56	£40,894.56
7	£5,472.00	£3,168.25	£38,304.00	£11,230.81	£49,534.81
8	£5,472.00	£3,792.86	£43,776.00	£15,023.67	£58,799.67
9	£5,472.00	£4,462.62	£49,248.00	£19,486.29	£68,734.29
10	£5,472.00	£5,180.79	£54,720.00	£24,667.08	£79,387.08
11	£5,472.00	£5,950.88	£60,192.00	£30,617.96	£90,809.96
12	£5,472.00	£6,776.64	£65,664.00	£37,394.60	£103,058.60
13	£5,472.00	£7,662.10	£71,136.00	£45,056.70	£116,192.70
14	£5,472.00	£8,611.56	£76,608.00	£53,668.26	£130,276.26
15	£5,472.00	£9,629.66	£82,080.00	£63,297.93	£145,377.93

Interest compounded **monthly**. Monthly deposits made at beginning of each compound period.

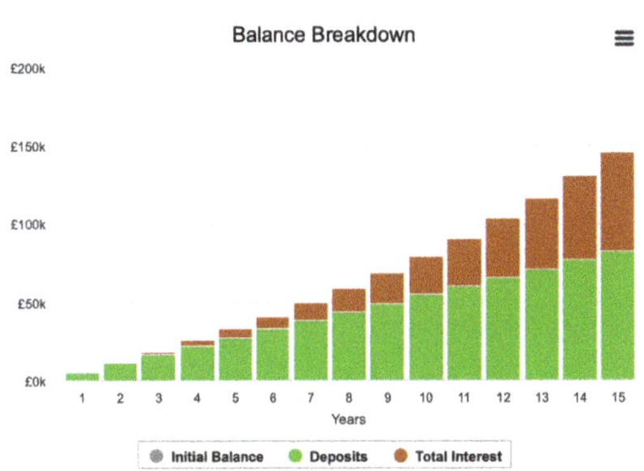

Figure 3. £15 saved daily over 15 years
Source: The Calculator Site **(bit.ly/32MxCZp)** [9]

Which makes sense; if you were a manager, wouldn't you prefer giving responsibility to someone who cared about the business rather than someone who clocked-off at 5pm regardless of what was about to hit the fan?

A word of advice: whatever you do, do not let your side hustle interfere with your day job. Do not abuse your company and its assets, e.g. telephones/computers/photocopiers/internet, and absolutely do not run your side business on your employer's time.

Here's an interesting link to a blog entitled 101 Ways To Get A Raise At Work (**bit.ly/3hrltxa**). Some of the comments are a bit cheesy, but it's fun and has plenty of worthwhile suggestions.

Finally, there is a book entitled Give and Take by Adam Grant that will help you appreciate how committing to your work and your responsibility to others helps your career, as well as all other relationships (see Resources, page **79**).

DO WHAT YOU LOVE VS LOVE WHAT YOU DO

By way of career guidance, social media tells us to "do what you love", as if success and happiness will automatically follow. No, it won't. At least not for the majority of us. There's nothing wrong whatsoever with doing what you love, but as a guiding career principle it just isn't very nuanced, nor particularly practical, advice.

Everyone has slightly different needs from their job. For some security is paramount, for others creative freedom is essential, and yet others crave promotions and the accompanying salary increases. Whatever your priorities, I would contend there is a higher correlation in meeting them by learning to love what you do, than doing what you love.

> **Success causes passion more often than passion creates success.**

LET ME BACK UP...

Establishing goals, creating detailed plans and timeframes are important, but in themselves do not produce results. It's our personal efforts in implementing those plans that produce the results. Sadly, for many, the reality of delivering on those individual actions – the ones that lead to real results – is dreadful (how many people do you know who maintain their lifestyle diet and exercise plans or New Year resolutions?). So, what's the solution?

9. I like the simplicity and elegance of this calculator. The simplicity is deceptive; it's very powerful and graphically informative.

Year	SIMPLE INTEREST			COMPOUND INTEREST			Difference
	Amount Reinvested	Annual Interest	Cumulative Value	Amount Reinvested	Annual Interest	Cumulative Value	
1	£5,000	£250	£5,250	£5,000	£250	£5,250	£0
2	£5,000	£250	£5,500	£5,250	£263	£5,513	£13
3	£5,000	£250	£5,750	£5,513	£276	£5,788	£38
4	£5,000	£250	£6,000	£5,788	£289	£6,078	£78
5	£5,000	£250	£6,250	£6,078	£304	£6,381	£131
6	£5,000	£250	£6,500	£6,381	£319	£6,700	£200
7	£5,000	£250	£6,750	£6,700	£335	£7,036	£286
8	£5,000	£250	£7,000	£7,036	£352	£7,397	£387
9	£5,000	£250	£7,250	£7,387	£369	£7,757	£507
10	£5,000	£250	£7,500	£7,757	£388	£8,144	£644
SKIP 20 YEARS							
31	£5,000	£250	£12,750	£21,610	£1,080	£22,690	£9,940
32	£5,000	£250	£13,000	£22,690	£1,135	£23,825	£10,825
33	£5,000	£250	£13,250	£23,825	£1,191	£25,016	£11,766
34	£5,000	£250	£13,500	£25,016	£1,251	£26,267	£12,767
35	£5,000	£250	£13,750	£26,267	£1,313	£27.580	£13,830
36	£5,000	£250	£14,000	£27,580	£1,379	£28,959	£14,959
37	£5,000	£250	£14,250	£28,959	£1,448	£30,407	£16,157
38	£5,000	£250	£14,500	£30,407	£1,520	£31,927	£17,427
39	£5,000	£250	£14,750	£31,927	£1,596	£33,524	£18,774
40	£5,000	£250	£15,000	£33,524	£1,676	£35,200	£20,200
VALUE after 40 years			£15,000			£35,200	£20,200

Table 2. Simple Interest vs Compound Interest £5,000 principal at 5% interest

The secret words here are sustainability/tenacity/perseverance. Life, careers and saving for financial wellbeing are all a long haul. If you want to achieve anything of meaning you're going to have to face making a continuous effort. It's a struggle (tell me about it!). Yet, once again, I contend finding the strength, continuity and coping with the struggle has the better probability of success if you focus on being good at something.

We all have a sense of what we're good at relative to others. If you focus on these proclivities you're more likely to get even better at them, which means you'll make yet more effort to learn about those skills to maintain your relative performance. In other words, your skills will compound, and pretty soon you'll become indispensable to your company. But first you must learn to love what you do, and that only comes from working in a profession where your more innate abilities are part of the process.

It's worth noting that to have a special skill doesn't require you to be an amazing graphic designer, software programmer or super salesperson. Just doing mundane tasks, but doing them well, can get you noticed. For example, do what you say you will do and do it when you say you'll do it (and if, for genuine reasons, you can't hit the deadline, tell your colleague(s) before the deadline arrives), be a completer-finisher, go the extra mile, have integrity and be committed. As a business owner friend of mine once told me: "If I need exceptional talent, I can always hire it. To run my business I just need good people to do their best."

The trick, of course, is to find an environment where your skills – whatever they may be – are acknowledged and appreciated. If you find yourself working for an organisation that neither recognises nor values your contribution, start looking for another job.

I'm not for one minute suggesting you become a highly skilled, but miserable, workaholic. Rather, the chances are if you're good at something you probably enjoy it, and that in turn feeds through into your willingness for sustainability, tenacity and perseverance.

Professional success translates into more choices. More choices lead to helping you meet your emotional needs and financial expectations.

THE BEST WORK IS NOT WHAT IS MOST DIFFICULT FOR YOU; IT IS WHAT YOU DO BEST.

Jean-Paul Sartre, French philosopher (1905-1980)

COMPOUNDING

We all think we understand what compounding means, but do we?

Compounding has become used in the vernacular to describe many things. If you want to lose weight, eat less and exercise – the effects will compound. If you want to learn something, read lots of books and your knowledge will compound. If you want to sustain a relationship, make time and invest in the other person – the benefits will compound, etc...

It's the same with investing, except it's easier! With investing, compounding doesn't ask anything of you – just to leave it alone to get on with its job.

But what exactly is compounding? Compounding is an exponential calculation, such that interest or investment returns get added to interest/returns, which gets added to interest/returns, until it takes on a life of its own and snowballs, gathering mass and speed all the time you don't touch it, i.e. don't withdraw and spend your investments.

Being an exponential calculation, we struggle to calculate the value of compounding after just a few iterations. And because we can't do the maths in our heads we're inclined to forget about its effect on our savings. Don't do that.

Compounding is not a miracle, it's an inevitable mathematical fact. Simple interest is calculated on the principal invested each year. Whereas compound interest is calculated on the principal plus the previous year's interest. In short...

Simple Interest = Interest on Principal

Compound Interest = Interest on Principal & Accumulated Interest

Table 2 illustrates the difference between simple interest (the one we reflexively calculate in our heads) and compound interest (the calculation we can't do in our heads). The investor in this example doesn't invest an additional £5,000 every year, they just let the initial £5,000 roll over each year.

You will also note from Table 2 how interest earned each year grows and accelerates with time, thanks to compounding. This is one of the key reasons I suggest you start investing as soon as you can. Having invested £5,000 in the example for Table 2, the difference between simple interest and compound interest is £20,200.

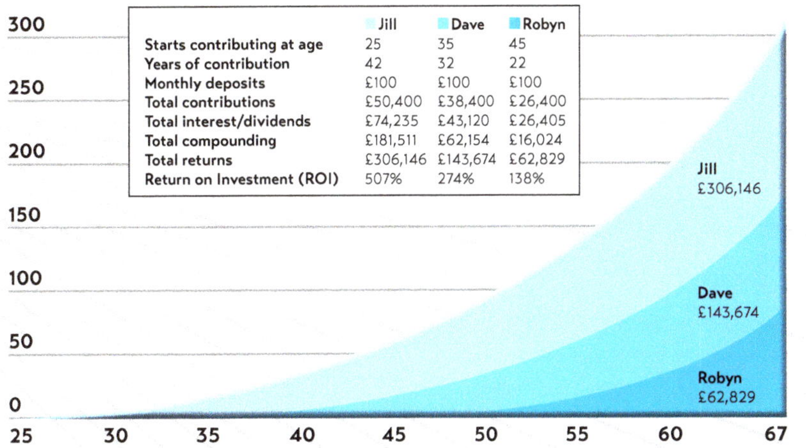

	Jill	Dave	Robyn
Starts contributing at age	25	35	45
Years of contribution	42	32	22
Monthly deposits	£100	£100	£100
Total contributions	£50,400	£38,400	£26,400
Total interest/dividends	£74,235	£43,120	£26,405
Total compounding	£181,511	£62,154	£16,024
Total returns	£306,146	£143,674	£62,829
Return on Investment (ROI)	507%	274%	138%

Figure 4.
The relationship between compounding and time with total nominal returns of 7%

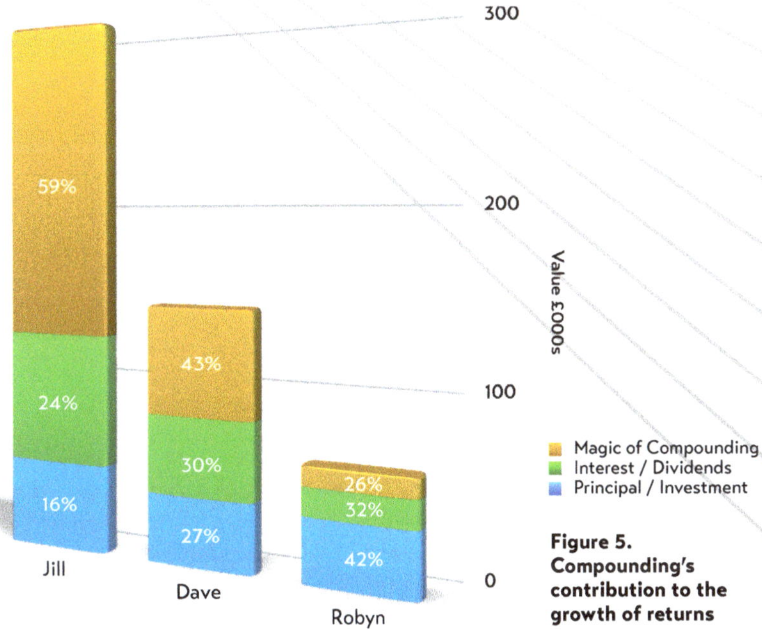

Figure 5.
Compounding's contribution to the growth of returns

Finally, and just to reinforce the importance of compounding's relationship to time, Figures 4 and 5 illustrate that relationship, and how giving compounding time boosts your returns.

Interestingly, based on Figure 4, in order to match Jill's final returns, Dave would have to invest £213 per month from age 35, while Robyn would have to invest £487 per month from age 45. If all three of them had invested £250 per month instead of £100 over the same periods, Jill, Dave and Robyn would have final returns of £765,366, £359,186 and £157,072, respectively.

If you use the online calculator identified in Figure 3 to calculate how the numbers in Figures 4 and 5 are derived, please note the numbers are compounded monthly, not yearly. This more accurately reflects the outcomes for Jill, Dave and Robyn who drip-feed their savings into their investments on a monthly basis.

For those of you who like a blended learning experience, here's an excellent vlog by Dave Ramsey (**bit.ly/3ipt7ec**) that makes numerous compelling points while demonstrating the power of compounding.

THE OPPORTUNITY COST OF YOUR DECISIONS

'Opportunity cost' is an economic term used to quantify the cost of making mutually exclusive decisions. For example, if someone decides to have a meal out before an interview the following morning, the opportunity cost of that decision is the lost time in preparing for the interview and the money spent on the meal that could have been spent on something else.

Thinking in terms of 'opportunity costs' is useful because it allows us to frame and evaluate our decisions. It's often instinctive, but not always.

In the above example, the lost time in preparing for the following morning's interview is unquantifiable, and therefore a judgement call. The money spent on the meal out is quantifiable and measurable. Both necessitate a decision you have to make: meal out or prepare for interview. Either way you can't undertake both activities simultaneously, and are thus faced with at least one 'lost opportunity.'

I have always had a passion for music. Even when I was living paycheque to paycheque, I spent money on buying music and decent kit to listen to it. I studied economics so I was well aware of the opportunity cost of funding my passion. Do I regret it now? No! Music has always made my life so much richer. The point is: you do not have to feel guilty about some of your spending decisions. You do not have to live the life of a pauper. On the other hand, it helps if you recognise the opportunity cost of those decisions before making them, and ask yourself if they're really worth it to you. If they are, then perhaps make sacrifices in other less important areas of your life.

PURCHASING DECISION	Annual cost	Opportunity cost after 25 years*
Netflix subscription (£8.99 pm)	£108	£7,080
£5 lunch every workday (230 days)	£1,150	£75,462
Two lattés every workday	£1,196	£78,486
One takeaway meal a week for four	£1,680	£110,244
£2,500 overseas holiday every year	£2,500	£164,053

Table 3. The opportunity cost of various quantifiable decisions measured against their value in terms of potential future investments (* based on 7% total nominal returns)

A NOTE ABOUT FIRE

FIRE is the acronym for **Financial Independence, Retire Early**. This movement started in the USA and has migrated to the UK. I can't say I'm a devotee. Those who follow the FIRE philosophy must be committed to extreme saving behaviours which, from my perspective, could lead to a less than fulfilling and meaningful lifestyle. Here's (**on.mktw.net/37HFGxP**) an interesting blog by someone who tried it.

However, horses for courses, and if you have a strong vision with a passion to match for reaching early retirement you might want to investigate here (**bit.ly/2HBigj5**).

FIRE may be for you. Just remember, it can be hard living a life so out of step with those of your peers who don't choose FIRE.

I know someone who followed FIRE. The sadness is that the reality of events eventually got in the way, and they found their savings were not enough to cope with such financial setbacks. To make matters worse, having been away from the job market for several years, they found it extremely tough securing a job for which they could be adequately rewarded.

Following a FIRE lifestyle is probably best suited to those who receive a significant inheritance early on, giving their investments a substantial boost. Alternatively, there are those professionals who have deliberately sought and accepted postings overseas in low tax regimes to speed their journey towards FIRE.

RECOGNISE AND EMBRACE MoTs

Learn to identify and embrace those times in your life when you can afford to start saving or to increase the sums you're already saving. They have been dubbed "Moments of Truth," or MoTs. Here are some examples:

- Paying off personal loans and/or credit card debt.
- Salary increases, perhaps through changing jobs or bonuses.
- Renegotiating better deals or switching your utilities, including telecomms.
- Reducing or refinancing your mortgage.
- Cancelling subscriptions you no longer really need.
- No longer having to pay childminder bills (or, at least, paying significantly less).
- Receiving an inheritance or a windfall.
- Moving in with your partner, thereby combining two salaries to run one home and pay only one set of bills.
- Paying less tax, due to tax code changes.

In each of the above cases the money you were spending now becomes available to save without impacting your lifestyle. You don't have to save all of the newly released money, but you could probably save a chunk of it.

VIDEO

Here's (**bit.ly/2HHXLkD**) a video about saving. It is presented by Kaillie Branciforte, someone I'd never heard of before researching this topic. Kaillie's short videos are thoughtfully structured, articulate and delivered with pace (so you won't be bored). More to the point, they are very helpful.

AN APP TO HELP YOU DEVELOP POSITIVE HABITS

If you like using technology on your mobile, here's an app that looks like fun. Productive (**bit.ly/2HJdCQ0**) helps you remember actions you wish to acquire on a regular basis, such as putting money aside for your savings. To learn how to use Productive go to ScreenCastsOnline (**bit.ly/3oDMblg**).

Finally, if you find yourself constantly missing your saving targets try The Behaviour Gap (**bit.ly/31Ttmai**) for guidance.

TAKEAWAY

Learn to recognise saving opportunities and act on them.

MY MoT FAILURE

Not long after my wife and I bought our first flat I was offered an opportunity to go and work in the Far East. I was given an 'expat deal' which meant our accommodation was included. That in turn meant we could rent out our flat in the UK while working overseas. In effect, the rent paid our mortgage. What we didn't do was invest the money we now had by not having to pay the mortgage or any rent. A lost MoT opportunity.

DEBT AND YOUR PRIORITIES

In thinking about making yourself debt-free, it helps to compare your expected investment returns with the interest you're paying on your debt. Bear in mind your long-term expected real investment returns are likely to be between 3.5% and 4.5% after inflation and costs. Some debt is more toxic than others, so, if you can, prioritise paying off the highest interest loans first. I would prioritise paying off debt charged above 6%.

When it comes to student debt you probably already know you don't have much choice. Once you reach a certain income (currently £26,575 per annum), your debt is deducted from your salary (see page **71**) by your employer, or, if you're self-employed, through your tax filing. The choice you do have, however, is whether to pay off the debt early.

Deciding which debt to pay off first is not always obvious, and the assumptions behind whether to pay off debt, or instead, to invest any savings, are not straightforward.

If you're wondering about juggling your priorities between building an emergency fund or paying off debt, getting rid of your especially toxic debt trumps the emergency fund. Aside from saving money, if you pay off your debt you will have a better credit score, and with a strong credit rating you can borrow money during times of an unexpected emergency.

The first thing to understand about debt is:

- Acceptable debt is low-interest and applied to buying things that appreciate in value, e.g. your home.
- Bad debt is high-interest and is used to buy things that depreciate (go down in value) over time, e.g new model cars.

The two most common approaches to paying off personal debt are the 'snowball' and the 'avalanche' methods. The snowball approach requires paying off your smallest debt first. This is not the financially smartest way to do it, but the theory is that you will get a buzz from achieving this easier goal and thus be inspired to carry on paying off your other debts. The avalanche system dictates you pay off your highest interest debt first. This is the financially astute way. My personal choice is the avalanche way, but you decide which approach gives you the greatest motivation.

To better understand which method to adopt, a simple yet excellent explanation is available at How to pay off debt by Marko of White Board Finance (**bit.ly/3oZNMbf**). In the second half of this YouTube video, Marko recommends and demonstrates a freely downloadable spreadsheet from Vertex42 available here (**bit.ly/3p115sg**). You will find an example of this spreadsheet in the Appendix on page **70**. There are also online debt calculators, such as those at Calculator.net (**bit.ly/2JIHvkg**).

However, you're not finished yet!

The issue you now need to address is this: at what point are you better off investing than paying down a particular debt? You may not need to prioritise paying off your mortgage as quickly as you can.[10] This is because in many instances you'll make more money from investing. Even so, given the uncertainty of predicting future investment returns, there's no one right answer. It all depends on the assumptions you make and the lifestyle you choose.

There is a vlog by Jennifer Kempson that helps explain, and gives examples, of the pay off debt or invest dilemma. It is available here (**bit.ly/3l3lzOp**). I like most of Jennifer's vlogs; they begin with a short introduction but swiftly get down to the nitty gritty – which is what really helps. Jennifer has her own website at MamaFurFur. During the vlog, Jennifer uses her own spreadsheet called the AutoPilotMoney (**etsy.me/2Gza6Hz**). It costs £19.72, but it does so much more than simply assist you in determining how to pay off debt. I bought it and it's a gem.

Jennifer makes the practical suggestion that perhaps you shouldn't pay down your debt as quickly as possible, but instead to use part of your ability to save to invest. Her argument is that if you begin to invest, even if only with very small amounts, you will start to acquire useful habits and understand the markets. That's a strong argument. Once again, the choice is yours. As you will shortly discover, maximising your employer's pension contribution is always worth it (see pages **40** and **68**).

In practice, you might consider making minimum payments on your mortgage and student loans, maxing-out your employer pension contribution, then using any excess savings you can make to dip your toes into the investment markets.

My favourite blogs/vlogs are by Pete Matthew of Meaningful Money. Here's a link to his podcast and video entitled The Ultimate Guide to Paying Off Debt (**bit.ly/3mVMIsL**). It is very thorough and compassionate, going so far as to identify specific charities you can contact if you feel you need one-on-one help with your debt issues. If you download Pete's workbook (freely available from the link above), Pete offers the following advice to those of you looking down a hole of debt and unable to climb out:

"It might be the case that when following the steps in this workbook and listening to the accompanying podcast, you realise that your debt problem is too big for you to fix on your own.

If you feel that you're never getting ahead, or even standing still, but instead are being dragged further and further behind by your debt, you need to seek help – and fast.

First, you should contact the Citizens' Advice Bureau at **www.citizensadvice.org.uk** Two debt relief charities you could consider are:

- Christians Against Poverty – **capuk.org**
- StepChange – **www.stepchange.org**

And finally, a company which is not a charity, but is free to the end-user because it is funded by donations from the debt industry is PayPlan – **www.payplan.com**"

Finally, on the subject of reducing your debt, it is worth mentioning that long-term debt, such as a mortgage or student debt, becomes less burdensome over time as a result of inflation. For example, if inflation runs at 2.5% each year, a £150,000 mortgage after 20 years becomes £90,400 in relative terms. At the same time, your salary – and thus, hopefully, your ability to save – increases (at least in tandem with inflation).

10. A useful article addressing the various issues surrounding whether or not to pay off your mortgage can be found here (**bit.ly/2Wu7vTt**).

THE EXCEPTIONS

Everybody's situation is different, but a few basic principles apply to everyone.

Following recent UK legislation, most private sector employees working in companies must now be auto-enrolled in a company pension,[11] and all employers must make a contribution towards that pension. Before paying off your debt, always max-out your personal pension contributions, in order to match your employer's maximum contribution. The return on your employer's contribution to your pension plan is worth a minimum of 40%, which is higher than even the worst credit card interest rate.[12]

If you are one of the lucky few with a defined benefit pension, aka a final salary scheme (nowadays largely only available to public sector employees), your decision is different. There's a reason why public sector pensions are known as 'gold-plated'. Public sector pensions are, on average and over time, worth three times more than anything available to those in the private sector [13] (who have defined contribution pension schemes). Thus, whatever your monthly contributions are, your pension will be worth at least three times more upon retirement than anything available to a private sector employee making the same payments. Furthermore, you will not have to endure the emotional rollercoaster of bull and bear markets.[14] Your pension will also be guaranteed by the government and will be index linked, which is to say, inflation-proofed. Public sector pensions are paid for by the many to the few. You really must take advantage of this munificence while it lasts, and that means maximising your contributions to take full advantage of your final pension plan benefits. Next, eliminate your credit card debt, followed by any loans, e.g. car or bank loans, but not necessarily your mortgage or student debt.

STUDENT LOANS

The rules surrounding UK student loans for tuition fees and maintenance grants are forever shifting.[15] Currently, you are automatically obliged to pay down your student loans once you reach a certain salary threshold. The more you earn the more you have to pay back. However, it's not that simple. The nature of your student debt is dependent on when you acquired it, as well as what type it was. To better understand how your student debt works go to money (**bit.ly/2IjUVCX**). An alternative website is The Student Room (**bit.ly/2IFn33a**). To establish how to pay off your student debt obligations, I recommend this calculator on Money Saving Expert (**bit.ly/2GFxZx9**).

Having spoken to a number of graduates, I realised there was some confusion as to the interest charged on their loans. Some thought it was 9%. This is not the case. The 9% figure is used to calculate how much of your salary above the threshold will be deducted from your income to repay your loan. It is not the interest on your loan!

If student debt is of interest to you, I have added a section in the Appendix: *Managing student debt*, available on page **71**. There, you will find I have identified some really helpful vlogs by the the UK's guru on the subject, Martin Lewis.

YOUR EXPECTED REAL RETURNS AFTER COSTS

The above paragraphs contain three significant inferences. Note I quoted your 'expected real returns' for your retirement savings at between 3.5% and 4.5%. For the moment we'll park how I arrived at this figure, but please recognise it's not a guarantee but an historical average.

The second significant inference relates to the use of the expression 'real return'. Real return has a very specific meaning when referring to investments. Real returns are those adjusted for inflation, as opposed to nominal returns, which are before inflation. Thus, if your investments returned 6% over a year and inflation was 2% during the same period, then your nominal returns would be 6% and your real returns would be 4%.

Inflation is a huge drag on investment performance and negatively impacts the eventual purchasing power of your savings. Nominal returns – except in deflationary economic environments – will always be higher than real returns. For this reason, the media and those touting investment products will invariably quote nominal returns. Always check what return label is being applied, and be savvy to the fact that nominal and real returns are very different. The ones that matter most to you are real returns.

Finally, the returns of 3.5% to 4.5% quoted above are also after all investment fees and charges. Most financial advisers, even if referring to after-inflation returns, will rarely state after-cost returns. Be wise to this.

11. You can opt out but I wouldn't advise it unless absolutely necessary.

12. Recent changes in the way banks charge for unauthorised overdrafts has resulted in some now charging fees approaching 40%. Be watchful.

13. Source: Tax Payers Alliance, Quantum Advisory (**bit.ly/3pliDhF**)

14. Those moments when the investment markets fall (bear market) and rise (bull market) rapidly and/or consistently in value.

15. Maintenance loans are amalgamated with your tuition fees, and this combined figure becomes your student debt. The amount of the maintenance grant to which a student is entitled is dependent on where they live and their parental income.

APPRECIATING THE BASICS OF FINANCIAL MARKET HISTORY

For many people investing is akin to gambling. However, everybody knows if you frequent the casino you will eventually lose all your money. The casino isn't cheating, it's simply that the rules set by The House and the mathematics of chance are designed to give the casino an edge. In short, the longer you play the roulette table, the more you will lose. Investing is the opposite; provided you follow a few simple rules, the longer you stay vested in the markets the more money you will make.

The four main, and simple, rules to successful investing are:

1. **Keep a diversified portfolio of investments.** Some of the funds recommended in MYFE Book 3 are already diversified for you, and will automatically rebalance your asset allocation and risk profile as you get older.
2. **Manage your investment costs.** Generally speaking, if you're 55 years old or younger and your all-in investment fees and costs exceed 1% you're paying too much.
3. **Do not withdraw the income from your investments, unless in a genuine emergency.** Reinvesting your returns turbocharges the growth of your investments.
4. **Don't panic by selling your holdings when markets tumble.** During your investment journey markets will tank, probably several times. And yet, diversified portfolios have always rebounded over time and gone on to new highs. Try to keep the faith.

Having a basic knowledge of how markets have performed over time will not only help you appreciate why the above four rules are crucial, but give you the confidence to stick with them.

A word of caution: just because you may become better informed about historical market cycles, never presume you can predict them. At any one point in time there will always be market commentators who are bullish or bearish about the next turn of events. Ignore them. No one, and I mean absolutely no one, has ever been able to consistently 'time' the markets. The key to your financial success rests in knowing **what matters most is time in the market, not timing the market**.

MYFE Book 2 will give you the additional historical evidence and knowledge to have the confidence to invest for the long term. Furthermore, it will demonstrate how and why some investors become wealthy, and others don't (who – were it not for their own behaviour – could have been).

Far more money has been lost by investors preparing for corrections, or trying to anticipate corrections, than has been lost in corrections themselves.

Peter Lynch, fund manager, author and philanthropist

PANDEMICS

Covid-19 will create untold hardship for many. Our hearts go out to them, especially those in developing nations whose healthcare and welfare support systems are virtually non-existent. For those of us in developed economies we can at least be thankful we are unlikely to starve. Everything is relative.

If you're one of the fortunate people with an investment portfolio you will nevertheless have recently experienced a couple of buttock-clenching moments. I have. Even so, in times of share price volatility, my advice is to do nothing. Yes, there will be those who make changes to their portfolio and profit from it. There will also be many who make changes and get it horribly wrong.

Will the markets recover? Yes. Why? Because, barring social unrest/war, climate catastrophes, more pestilence, solar storms, comet collisions or alien invasion, history tells us they always do, and because people the world over are resilient and resourceful. The question isn't 'if', it's 'when'.

Whatever the severity and duration of the current crisis, there will doubtless be much share market volatility and perhaps several false dawns, known as bear market rallies.

Nevertheless, it's worth remembering that since the 1930s, USA bear markets have lasted on average only 18 months. The average time it's taken for a portfolio of shares to both endure a bear market and fully recover its value has been just over three years.

Eventually markets will rebound. As Millennials or Generation X, you have a good 10 to 30 years before needing to access your investment funds, so you have the time to wait for markets to recover. An interesting article by the asset management firm Schroders on stock market recoveries can be found here **(bit.ly/2WMEYs0)**.

So, what are the prospects for Millennials and Generation X exiting lockdown? Doubtless job markets and personal incomes will become tighter, making it harder to reach your financial expectations. With this in mind, you may want to visit one or all of the three major blogs for financial ideas and advice; they are:

- Money Saving Expert **(bit.ly/31rLVCn)**
- Money to the Masses **(bit.ly/2FPFBw8)**
- Be clever with your cash **(bit.ly/3jd41Ox)**

All three websites have extensive archives, so if you can't see what you're looking for immediately, try searching by topic. They offer practical advice on special promotions, financial regulations and tax, mortgages and loans, as well as initiatives for budgeting, saving and investing.

If you're thinking of retraining, a useful website can be found at **nationalcareers.service.gov.uk**.

The Rebel Business School **(bit.ly/3j2v2pp)** is a free resource to guide you on how to start/grow a small business. Due to Covid, events are currently being held online as at the time of writing this book.

I have loitered on the topic of Covid-19 and the current state of the investments markets because many will be convinced now is the time to sell their investments before even greater damage is done. Whatever the crisis du jour, there will always be the doomsayers. It's important therefore to remember...

The four most dangerous words in investing are 'It's different this time.'

Sir John Templeton, legendary investor

UNDERSTANDING THE MECHANICS OF INVESTING

The innovations and regulations surrounding the investment markets and their tax ramifications are constantly evolving. Trying to navigate your way through the financial markets without knowing where to look is like trying to sail across an ocean without a compass. It can be done, but I wouldn't recommend it.

You will therefore need an adequate understanding of how today's financial markets work. Just some of the questions you need to get sorted from the off are:

- How to measure and evaluate investment fees and costs.
- What each of the four investment return measures mean, and which one is most important to you.
- Which tax wrappers are best suited to your individual financial goals and their time horizons.
- What protection the government offers.
- What products should be avoided.
- What online platform(s) to use when investing and monitoring your investments.

You don't need a degree on the subject, far from it. But you do need to know the basics. Books 2 and 3 will teach you what you need to know.

AVOIDING THE MONEY GRABBERS

I started writing Managing Your Financial Expectations shortly after I had been duped by an Independent Financial adviser (IFA). It wasn't the first time. I was fed up and didn't want my own millennial kids to experience the same aggravation.

The trouble with financial charlatans is that they're hard to spot; after all, their most important talent is charm. These individuals are aware most people know next to nothing about the financial markets and are easily impressed by those who appear to be more knowledgeable and employ confusing terminology while displaying impressive-looking charts. What's more, there's really little to be gained from asking for client references – who's going to give you a list of disgruntled clients?

You can, of course, ask family and friends for personal recommendations, but be careful. Your family and friends could themselves be investing with a less than up-front financial adviser without knowing.

I'm afraid there is only one effective way to identify the overly avaricious when seeking a financial adviser, and that's to arm yourself with some knowledge, hence the MYFE books.[16]

Please try to sidestep the relative or friend who is a financial adviser themselves. Over time you may be forced to ask some difficult questions, and the ultimate cost may be a relationship you hold dear.

The question of how to select a financial adviser that's right for you is not easy. Such relationships are best approached as long term, and as such require serious thought. I have found searching the internet for such assistance relatively unhelpful. I will be posting a special and detailed article on MYFE.guide addressing this specific issue (just leave an email in the 'Subscribe for updates' section to be notified when it's available).

It would, however, be unwise and unfair to judge and condemn all intermediaries. There are many financial services professionals who care passionately about the social value and integrity of their industry, and service their clients honourably. The trick is finding them, and matching your needs to their standards.[17]

MANAGING YOUR OWN BEHAVIOUR

When you first start your investment journey you'll doubtless be underwhelmed by the returns. Returns of 3.5% to 4.5% (after inflation and costs) grow slowly. That is until the wonder of compounding really kicks-in (after approximately 20 years), at which point you'll be walking around with a permanent grin.[18]

There is, however, one exception: every so often you will be confronted with moments of high anxiety, which, if you fail to temper your natural inclinations, will destroy your investments. These moments occur during periods of high stock market volatility, causing you intense stress when markets fall.

Human beings are not hardwired to handle long-term risk. Over the millennia we've been on this planet we've been conditioned to see risk as a short-term phenomenon. In other words, when confronted with danger our instincts are either flight or fight. When faced with falling markets these instinctive responses translate into either selling our investments before we lose anymore (flight), or move our investments into the latest fad being promoted by the media (fight). The truly successful investor knows both these responses are misguided.

16. **MYFE Book 3** has a chapter, If It Waddles It's A Duck, identifying specific investment providers and products to avoid.

17. At this stage of your journey, however, your need for a financial adviser is limited. Furthermore, if your investments add up to less than £60,000 most advisers are likely to want to be paid by the hour (the average cost is £200ph), instead of a 1% fee.

18. Albert Einstein is said to have referred to the inevitable mathematics of compounding as, 'The eighth wonder of the world.'

You might think you can handle market volatility, but think again. It's all very well losing 40% of your savings when you're 35 and you've got £1000 at stake. But if after 20 years of hard graft you find yourself with a share portfolio of £250,000, which then drops to £150,000 in the next bear market, that's a whole different world of emotions.

The best solution is simple: do nothing. As I said, simple but not easy. Sadly, too many people panic when confronted with a bear market. By selling their holdings and crystallising their losses it becomes impossible for their portfolio to recover.

What's more, if these investors had only taken a moment to read about historical market performance, they would realise markets don't stay down for long before bouncing back. The FTSE 250 Total Return index recovered within three years from the credit crunch of 2007/8, and went on to reach new highs. As Barney of The Escape Artist[19] puts it: "Stockmarket volatility is like a rollercoaster. If you stay strapped in, its harmless fun. But if you get out halfway through the ride, YOU'RE SCREWED."

No one can predict when, or often even know why, markets rise and fall. They don't do it in a consistent manner. Forecasting the specific week, let alone which day, when markets will rise or fall is a dangerous game, and I don't recommend it (unless, of course, you think you're more clairvoyant than anyone else on the planet). As explained previously, it isn't a matter of timing markets, but time in the markets that counts. Table 4 makes the point that staying vested is the better decision if you're in for the long haul. Missing just the best five days over a twenty six year period can reduce your gains by over 30%. If you missed all 40 days out of 6,738 you would have actually lost £6,649 of your initial investment, a return of minus 66%.

WHEN TO SEEK ADVICE

We all respond to financial setbacks in different ways, and our approach to risk varies. If you're unsure how you would respond in the above scenario and fear you might be prone to panic, go find a financial adviser to hold your hand. It'll cost you roughly 1% more in fees, but if your adviser can help you avoid making precipitous mistakes, they will have repaid their fees many times over.

Missing just a few days does deliver a large proportion of your portfolio gains. On the other hand, it's also true that missing a few of the worse performing days will actually provide an even better return (the worse days have a tendency to fall further than the best days rise). The challenge, of course, is being able to predict when the best and the worse days will occur. The problem is exacerbated by the fact the best and worse days frequently happen within close proximity to each other, known as volatility clustering. Even professional investors riveted to the markets fail to forecast these fluctuations with any consistency. We have no chance. So, provided you're happy with your portfolio mix of assets,[20] your best option is therefore to stay invested.

A successful investment strategy is essentially like watching grass grow. The first investment skill you need to acquire, therefore, is patience. The only way I've managed to sustain such patience is to read a few quality investment books/blogs. Throughout all the MYFE books I make recommendations to some of the best investment books published. While you're waiting for your money to grow, read them. This will be some of the most profitable reading you will ever do. It may not be too much of an exaggeration to suggest, in fact, that your financial life depends on it.

£10,000 INVESTED IN THE FTSE 350 INDEX	FTSE 350 Annualised Returns	Value of £10,000 at the End of the Period	Gain/Loss
All 6738 Trading Days	4.65%	£20,690	£10,690
Less the 5 days with the biggest gains	2.02%	£13,772	£3,772
Less the 10 days with the biggest gains	0.39%	£10,650	£650
Less the 20 days with the biggest gains	-2.30%	£6,888	-£3,112
Less the 40 days with the biggest gains	-6.61%	£3,351	-£6,649

Table 4. Missing The Best Days of the FTSE 350 Nominal Returns (share price movements only) from 1995 to October 2020
Source: Refinitiv Datastream

19. The Escape Artist is a fabulous website/blog. One of my favourites (see pages **50** & **78**).

20. How to determine the right asset mix for your personal goals and risk tolerance is a subject covered in MYFE Books 2 & 3.

There is one more emotion all investors must learn to put a lid on, namely greed. Greed, along with its sibling FOMO (Fear Of Missing Out), can be ruinous for investors. Obviously, we all want to achieve the maximum returns, but excessive greed frequently leads to unwarranted risk. Sadly, it is often those who come to recognise too late their need to save and invest, who forlornly attempt to catch up by taking inappropriate risks.

DON'T KID YOURSELF

Managing your financial expectations is not a matter of chance. It isn't just that you will need to curtail your instinctive behaviours when markets tumble, you will also have to acknowledge that saving and investing is a long-haul proposition. It requires self-sacrifice and practice. It is because so many people fail to appreciate the personal commitment required to meet their financial expectations that they fail to achieve financial wellbeing.

The fashionable mantra that it's best to 'live in the now' is good advice on many levels. But when it comes to managing your finances it's not.

The hard reality is that unless you spend time now planning your savings and investments for tomorrow, your tomorrow will suck and give you so many more headaches.

Financial planning is a chore and it's difficult. It's a chore because it requires time and learning new skills. It's difficult because it necessitates tenacity, as well as the self-restraint and energy to stay focused on your long-term objective. But you MUST do it.

Financial planning is a mental and emotional marathon. The secret is to hold onto the vision, and occasionally treat yourself to imagining how good you will feel as you reach your destination.

ONE LAST THING...

When I was in my thirties my peers and I felt immortal. Problem was, we weren't.

- If you have the possibility of acquiring a genetically inheritable disease or you're self-employed and work in an accident-prone industry, and you have regular financial commitments, please consider critical illness cover or income protection insurance.
- If you own a property you should insure it, and make sure it includes homeowner's liability cover.
- If you have a young family think about life insurance.

The point is: s**t happens, and you need to protect yourself and your loved ones.

Probably the best video podcast I've come across that discusses your income insurance options is by Pete Matthew, author of The Meaningful Money Handbook. You can find his podcast here (**bit.ly/2L4mqht**).

If you want to get competitive quotes for various types of insurance, a good place to start is **LifeSearch.com**.

Don't buy too much insurance. Insurance is an expense, not an investment. It's not an alternative to accomplish your investment goals, and it can't replace an emotional loss. Buy just enough to cover your needs. Don't allow yourself to be persuaded to use a life policy as an investment. At least wait until you've read MYFE Book 3 and are better informed about potentially more cost-efficient investments.

Finally, make a will and make sure your pension beneficiaries are named in it. Additionally, make sure your pension scheme administrator is equally aware of their name(s) too. Do not let those you care for, or those for whom you are responsible, suffer the additional delay and anguish of intestate. A useful and cost-efficient website for enacting a valid will can be found at **Farewill**.

To be really organised about your affairs, you might want to visit Once I've Gone. (**bit.ly/3vRJyWp**)

You must put in energy, effort, and belief into your goals every day before you can become what others call 'lucky'.

Kingsley Grant, author and inspirational speaker

MY STORY

My wife and I had three children and a mortgage. Both of us paid for critical illness insurance. Neither of us had any family history of genetic or other illnesses. Nevertheless, we felt it prudent to pay for such insurance in case something happened. It did.

Our son mentioned he had headaches and feelings of nausea first thing in the morning. He also began struggling to read the blackboard at school. We took him to see his GP several times, and each time were told it's nothing but sinuses, not to worry, he'd soon get over it. The problems persisted. By chance a follow-up appointment with a paediatrician was with a locum who immediately realised something more may be amiss. This locum asked the same questions of our son. Our son is neither a dramatist nor a complainer, and this exceptional doctor listened to his low-key answers and took them seriously. Without hesitation she organised an MRI scan for the next day and an ambulance to take him to London (this wonderful lady must have used a lot of her persuasive skills to secure a next-day MRI scan). In the unimaginable terror of the moment I never did remember her name – but wherever you are, THANK YOU, you saved our son's life.

The scan revealed our son had a brain tumour the size of a golf ball.

The NHS were magnificent, and the nurses unbelievably devoted and caring. After a seven-hour operation, the neurosurgeon, Chris Chandler of King's College Hospital, advised us the tumour had been removed, but couldn't say yet whether it was malignant or benign. He also warned us it was impossible to say what lasting side effects there might be of such extensive brain surgery.

Please bear with me, I will get to why this is relevant for critical illness insurance in a moment. In the meantime, allow me to write a few words I need to say and, more importantly, thank some quietly heroic people.

Our son was in hospital for three weeks. During this time my wife and I never left his side, taking it in turns to sleep in our car in the hospital carpark – that is until a nurse saw our situation and introduced us to Ronald McDonald House Charities UK, an independent non-profit family and children's charity supported by McDonald's. The charity's mission is to offer a home away from home to families with sick children in their time of need.

At a time when our world seemed to be falling apart, Ronald McDonald Houses gave my wife and me a free ensuite room for two weeks. It made such a difference: a better sleep and shower gave us both more strength and fortitude to support our son and family. Large corporations get a lot of flak, so we would like to say a big thank you to this exceptional charity, McDonald's, including its franchisees and their staff, as well as a special thanks to all of you reading this book who give to Ronald McDonald House Charities UK while treating yourself at McDonald's.

Thankfully, the tumour was benign. The side effects, whilst not life-shattering in the long run, were nonetheless painful and limiting in the short term. Our son had quadruple vision and his left arm shook when extended.

I have lived and worked on four continents, and one of the things I missed most while overseas was the British sense of humour. For many it is deemed wicked, if not cruel, but if it comes from those who are true friends it's a powerful expression of affection.

For example, even after a couple of years, and given my son's left arm shook uncontrollably, his mates showed him no mercy. He told us, while laughing himself, how his friends would make him get the first round of drinks at the pub. Trouble was by the time he brought the pints back to the table he'd spilled most of them. His mates immediately told him to go back and buy another round to make up for the spillage. Wicked but funny, and very British.

It's important to note, however, these were the same mates who: spent their own pocket money on not inexpensive train fares to visit him in hospital; who, when he came home, always checked to see if he wanted to go out, and made damn sure at least one of them was available to accompany him; who sat with him for hours. Great mates. Our son is lucky, on so many levels.

We had yet to face many bureaucratic hurdles of which we were blissfully unaware. We would have been lost without the tireless efforts and constant smiles of Elizabeth Goda, Mr Chandler's administrator. We had no idea of the paperwork involved after a serious brain operation: school boards, travel documents, motorbike licences, special insurances, detailed medical reports to name a few. Given our state of mind at the time, we would have struggled without Liz's help.

HERE'S THE POINT

Unbeknownst to us until a friend mentioned it, many critical illness policies include a lump sum payout if the policyholder's children have a major medical issue. So, having submitted all the necessary reports in the right formats to the right departments (thank you, Liz!), my wife and I each received a five-figure sum.

We gave this to our son who, to his everlasting credit and our great pride, immediately donated a chunk of it to the favoured charity supported by the real hero of the hour, Chris Chandler. Our son was well aware if it hadn't been for the courage, dedication and skill of Mr Chandler, he wouldn't be here.

I wouldn't wish this experience on anyone. But the 'takeaway' from my family's overwhelming moment is that life throws curve balls at many of us, we just don't know when, where or how. Taking prudent and appropriate insurance can help soften the blow when it does. In our case, it wasn't required to keep the family financially afloat, but it did make a big difference to a young man who went through a very tough time.

Our son is now 35, married and fit as a fiddle.

Ronald McDonald House Charities United Kingdom

To donate to this amazing charity please go here. (bit.ly/3fbu5u3)

PART **TWO**

People do not decide their futures, they decide their habits and their habits decide their futures.

F. Matthias Alexander, who developed techniques for overcoming reactive and habitual behavioural limitations

SAVING AND INVESTING TAX-EFFICIENTLY

So, how do you implement the overall plan that we've addressed in Part One?

As we have seen, your first priority is to get yourself out of debt. Until then, the only investing you should undertake is to maximise your employer pension match.

Next, you'll need to establish an emergency fund. This money should not be invested in the markets, but held in deposit accounts or cash ISAs, or a combination of both. The point here is to make your rainy-day fund easily accessible and not to put its value at risk.

A safe place to keep your emergency fund is at National Savings & Investments **(NS&I)**. It is effectively Government-backed and often has better rates than bank deposit accounts. Your money is relatively accessible (it takes two days to transfer your savings into your bank account). A couple of short and interesting articles on how to establish an emergency fund can be found at The Evidence-Based Investor (**bit.ly/3lznKdm**) and Conversation of Money (**bit.ly/2QPJneC**). As Pete Komolafe states in Conversation of Money, a big financial goal is really a series of smaller goals. Please retain this piece of wisdom when you start saving for your emergency fund, it's so true.

Another resource by Vanguard to better understand how to tackle your emergency fund can be found here (**bit.ly/3fskL5F**). Make sure to read the feedback comments at the bottom, they add depth to the article.

Then, and only then, when you've established your emergency fund, are you ready to invest your additional savings.

DEALING WITH BUDGETS

Budgeting is one of the fundamental ways of establishing how much you can afford to save/invest (see page 55 for useful resources). Budgets are important, and you should try to create one for yourself at least once, and try to revisit it annually. The problem with budgets is they're a faff, and I honestly don't know many people who keep them constantly updated.

My suggested solution is to keep tabs on your monthly expenditures, and if you find your bank balance can't afford your spending habits... change them! Keep prioritising what's genuinely important to you, avoid impulse purchases and cutback your expenses until you've managed to generate a monthly surplus. Then invest that surplus. It sounds simple, yet it works (but only if you want it to!).

Helpful links for budgeting can be found here (bit.ly/3qGqIP5). This is a great blog by Jason Butler aimed at those new to saving and investing, and written with empathy. Jason's stated goal is to 'make money simple' for all of us.

TAXES

You cannot control the direction of the investment markets. But you can, and must, control the costs you pay to invest in them. Therefore, it is reasonable to view taxes as one of your costs. Investing in the markets gives rise to tax. The three common taxes apply to: interest income, dividend income and capital gains.

YOUR TAX RATE

Before explaining how to legitimately shelter your various investments from tax, it's important to understand the basis on which we are taxed, and the personal allowances we're given. When saving and investing there are two components of the tax regime you need to know: tax on income and tax on investment income, i.e. your savings and investments.

Included overleaf is a quick summary of the various personal allowances available to you, together with the tax rates applied to your investments. The rates are slightly different for those living in Scotland and can also be found on the next page. Finally, an excellent explanation of personal taxes can be found here (**bit.ly/3dAVa8h**) at MoneySavingExpert.

TAX BAND	EARNINGS	TAX RATE	DIVIDEND RATE
Personal Allowance	**Up to £12,570**	0%	0%
Basic Rate	**£12,571 to £50,270**	20%	7.5%
Higher Rate	**£50,271 to £150,000**	40%	32.5%
Additional Rate	**Over £150,000**	45%	38.1%

Table 5.
UK Personal Income Tax Rates as at April 2021
Source: UK Government (gov.uk/income-tax-rates)

YOUR MARGINAL RATE OF TAX

Your marginal rate of tax is that at which your last £1 of income is taxed. For example, if you earned a salary of £12,671 or £50,370 your marginal tax rate would be 20% and 40%, respectively. This doesn't mean your entire salary is taxed at the marginal rate, just the amount which falls into the higher tax bracket. In the examples given, the marginal rate applies to the last £100 only. When calculating your marginal tax rate, your earned income and pensions are treated as the first 'slice' of income. The next slice is investment income, such as interest or rental income. Finally, any dividend income is treated as the top slice of your income.

Knowing your marginal rate of tax is not just important for establishing your net income, but influences the personal allowances to which you're entitled. A helpful online calculator for establishing your current or future tax and net salary can be found at The Salary Calculator (**bit.ly/2QA8mip**).

PERSONAL ALLOWANCES

The Government allows us all what they call 'personal allowances'. Personal allowances give you an amount of income you can receive before any tax is taken.

INTEREST AND DIVIDEND ALLOWANCES

In addition to your personal allowances there are further tax-free allowances for both interest income and dividends.

For a basic rate taxpayer, the first £1,000 of interest income is tax-free. This reduces to £500 for a higher rate taxpayer and is zero for additional rate taxpayers.

An additional tax-free 'savings allowance' is available to those individuals whose interest income falls in the tax band from £12,570 to £17,570.

The first £2,000 of dividend income is also tax-free and this is the case regardless of your marginal tax rate.

How to calculate your tax on dividend income can be found here (**bit.ly/3k9HwKS**).

The rules and regulations regarding savings and investments are not straightforward. For further information please visit UK Government (**bit.ly/2ZvV2kf**).

ANTICIPATED CHANGES TO TAX REGULATIONS

With the extent of Government borrowing to support the economy during the Coronavirus pandemic, it is anticipated changes will be made to the tax regime to allow the Government to recoup its borrowings.

Doubtless, if and when such changes happen, the media will be all over them. Please make sure you keep yourself up to date, as they may impact many of the allowances highlighted in the tables below.

CAPITAL GAINS TAX (CGT)

If you sell an asset, such as shares in a company, that has risen in value since you bought it, you will be exposed to Capital Gains Tax (CGT) on the difference between what it cost initially and the price at which you sell it, your gain. Your CGT tax-free allowance is £12,300 for the tax year 2020/21 (up from £12,000 in 2019/20). If some sales result in a loss, the loss is deducted from any gains you made in the same tax year. Furthermore, losses incurred in the previous 4 years can be brought forward and used against current year gains.

PERSONAL ALLOWANCES

EARNINGS	PERSONAL ALLOWANCE
Under £100,000	£12,570
£100,000 to £125,140	Decreases from £12,570 by £1 for every £2 you earn over £100,000 until it reaches £0
Over £125,140	£0

INVESTMENT TAXES

TAX BAND	DIVIDEND TAX
Basic Rate Taxpayers	7.5%
Higher Rate Taxpayers	32.5%
Additional Rate Taxpayers	38.1%
TAX BAND	**CAPITAL GAINS TAX**
Annual exempt amount	£12,300
Standard (Basic) CGT Rate	18% on residential property and 10% on other assets
Higher and Additional CGT Rate	28% on residential property and 20% on other assets

TAX RATES FOR THOSE LIVING IN SCOTLAND

Under your personal allowance (PA) for most, £12,570	No income tax payable
Between PA and PA + £2,097 (starter rate) for most, over £12,570 to £14,667	19%
Between PA + £2,097 and PA + £12,726 (basic rate) for most, over £14,667 to £25,296	20%
Between PA + £12,726 and PA + £31,092 (intermediate rate) for most, over £25,296 to £43,662	21%
Between PA + £31,092 and £150,000 (higher rate) for most, over £43,662 to £150,000	41% (1)
Over £150,000 (additional rate)	46%
Personal allowance drops by £1 for every £2 earned over £100,000	

Source: MoneySavingExpert

TAX WRAPPERS

Fortunately, the Government offers several legitimate alternatives for shielding our savings and investments from tax, while also allowing them to grow free of tax. The main mechanisms whereby we are legally able to reduce taxes are called 'tax wrappers.' Tax wrappers offer investors protection from tax if they 'wrap' their investments within a specific legal structure. Inevitably, all tax wrappers come with conditions.

The two common tax wrappers you need to consider are pensions and ISAs. Pensions and ISAs each have distinct compliance and tax regulations. Which tax wrapper you use depends on your financial goals and when they materialise.

Using either a pension or ISA allows your investments to grow free of interest tax, dividend tax[21] and capital gains tax. In other words, the money you would have paid in tax remains in your portfolio and helps it to grow. That's a big deal, particularly once compounding is taken into consideration.

PENSIONS

If you invest any money in a pension, you will not be able to access it until, at least, the age of 55 (recently announced regulatory changes will raise it to age 57 from 2028, see Heads Up! on page **43**). However, to encourage you to invest in a pension, the Government will 'top-up' the amount you invest to the tune of the basic rate of tax, 20%. Higher rate taxpayers are entitled to additional relief.

The Government encourages you to make pension contributions by offering full tax relief at your marginal tax rate. If you're a basic rate taxpayer (20%), the Government will deposit its 20% contribution directly into your pension, be it an employer pension or SIPP.[22] If you're a higher rate taxpayer (40%) the Government will deposit the first 20% directly into your pension, but the balance of 20% is claimed directly through your Self Assessment tax return.

Everyone, including low and non-earners, can invest in a pension. As will be revealed shortly, it is the tax advantaged amount you can invest that is regulated.

CALCULATING YOUR GOVERNMENT TOP-UP

It is commonly assumed that, if you're paying tax at 20%, for every £100 you invest in your pension the Government top up will be £20, giving you a total pension relief of £120. Not so. The Government top up in this example is £25.

21. If you do not use a tax-advantaged account you will pay dividend tax each year on your equity investments. Here's a useful dividend tax calculator from Which? (**bit.ly/39aJDvx**).

22. Self Invested Personal Pension: a pension you can access through many online investment platforms, and into which you can contribute and from where you select the funds to invest in and are able monitor your pension's performance. This all sounds complicated, but isn't. **Book 3** explains how it's done. Meanwhile, a useful explanation can be found at The Money Advice Service (**bit.ly/2EWq39O**).

PENSION TOP-UP EXPLAINED

Tax will already have been taken from your earned income, which the Government promptly returns to you in its top-up. Thus, as a 20% taxpayer, to make a £100 contribution to your pension you will have had to earn £125 before tax. The Government assumes, therefore, your £100 contribution is net of 20% tax, and thus only 80% of the total to which you're entitled. See the Appendix, Calculating your pension contribution, on page 68.

Your pension administrator will automatically receive your basic tax top-up. For higher and additional rate taxpayers, you will need to claim a refund of the balance of your marginal tax top-up when filing your tax returns, located on page TR4 of the SA100 tax return form.

The Government will 'give back' any excess above the 20% to which you're entitled by lowering your tax for the year.

It is always worth joining an employer's pension scheme. On the assumption this is part of an 'auto-enrolment' scheme, you will have to pay in 5% of your income between specified band earnings (for 2019-20 these are earning between £6,136 and £50,000), but your employer will also be required to pay a minimum of 3%. When combined with your tax relief, this represents a very substantial immediate return on your investment. Deciding to opt out of a workplace pension is like turning down a pay rise for doing no extra work.

EXAMPLE OF EMPLOYER CONTRIBUTION

If your employer matches your pension contribution up to 5% of your salary, and you earned £40,000 in total, you would maximise your employer's contribution at £2,000 (£40k x 5%). Your total pension investment in that year would therefore be £4,500, made up as follows:

- Your contribution of £2,000
- The Government contribution to your pension of £500
- Your employer match of £2,000

That's an epic instant return of 125%! [23]

Calculating the benefit of a company pension contribution is not intuitive. In Table 6 (below) you will find some additional examples.

If you are able to contribute more to your pension, and whether or not you decide to contribute more than your employer match, should depend on the underlying quality of your company pension scheme.

There are three issues to consider with company pensions:

1. The quality and type of funds into which your money is placed.
2. The underlying costs.
3. The asset allocation of your 'default' portfolio, i.e. the automatic asset mix into which the pension administrators will invest your funds. Frequently, and especially for Millennials, the default portfolio is too conservative, and leads to less than optimal returns.

You will need to ask your Human Resources or Treasury departments for details of the above three components of your company pension plan. Don't be shy, it is your absolute right to know the answers – it's your money and your future!

INVESTING IN YOUR EMPLOYER'S COMPANY

I would advise against investing in the shares of the company for which you work. You are already investing and risking your career with the company – that's enough. Those employees of Enron, a huge USA energy company, were aggressively encouraged by their management to invest in the company. It went bust in 2002, and its share price fell from a peak of $90.75 to $0.26. Many Enron employees lost their entire pensions. In the UK, over the last decade the list of big brand companies going bankrupt includes: Toys R Us, Borders, BHS, Staples, Blockbuster, Maplin, Tie Rack, Poundworld,

A very useful income tax and pension contribution calculator by MoneySavingExpert can be found here. (**bit.ly/3rXbMft**)

23. To learn how to calculate your investment returns please see the Appendix, page **69**.

TAX BAND	Zero	Basic	Higher	Additional
Your marginal tax rate	0%	20%	40%	45%
Earned income	£12,000	£35,000	£75,000	£160,000
Individual contribution	£600	£1,750	£3,750	£8,000
Government basic rate tax top-up	£150	£438	£938	£2,000
Employer contribution	£600	£1,750	£3,750	£8,000
Total amount added to your pension	£1,350	£3,938	£8,438	£18,000
Higher and Additional rate tax relief	£0	£0	£938	£2,500
Total benefit	£1,350	£3,938	£9,375	£20,500
Your Instant return on investment (ROI)	125%	125%	150%	156%

Table 6. Additional examples of employee/employer pension contributions

These examples assume the individual taxpayer's only source of income is from employment, and the individual employee contributes 5% of their gross income which is matched by their employer.

Glossary **of investment terms (bit.ly/3sCRxUO)**

Barratts, Phones4U, Debenhams, while many other companies now face tenuous futures as a result of Coronavirus.

If you feel you must be diplomatic and show faith, then only invest a little.

SALARY SACRIFICE

Many companies offer employees a 'salary sacrifice scheme' when it comes to pensions. To participate in such a scheme, you give up part of your salary (your sacrifice), which your employer then pays into your pension, along with their contribution to the scheme. The benefits of such an arrangement are:

- An automatic NIC saving up to 12% for the individual and 13.8% for the employer.
- Tax relief at the marginal rate is given automatically. There's no need to make a separate claim on your Self Assessment form.
- This will reduce your 'gross earnings'. This can have a beneficial impact: for example, where an individual's total income exceeds £50,000 and they are suffering a clawback of child benefit.

These schemes may be of particular interest to Generation X readers whose salaries have increased and/or where children have flown the nest and the everyday expenses of parenting are reduced, thus allowing them to save more.

If you can afford to take a lower salary and wish to increase your pension contributions, ask your employer if they offer this as part of their scheme. The attraction to the employer is a saving of 13.8% employer's NIC, and they may even be willing to share this with you. That said, there are potential downsides to salary sacrifice schemes, so I recommend you read this article (**bit.ly/341socb**) from Monevator.com before making any decisions.

GOING OUTSIDE YOUR EMPLOYER PENSION

The good news is that if you don't wish to invest additional savings into your company pension scheme beyond your employer match, the rules allow you to invest any additional pension entitlements elsewhere. You can invest either up to the total of your salary or £40,000 in any one year, whichever comes first. You may also be eligible to bring forward any unused relief from the previous three years.[24]

SEEK ADVICE

Pensions and the associated tax regulations are not straightforward and change regularly. Indeed, pensions are notoriously confusing at the best of times. The above basic examples cover common situations. If you are a higher or additional rate taxpayer, self-employed or have special issues, I strongly urge you to seek professional advice from an accountant or financial adviser before making any final decisions.

DON'T FALL INTO THE TRAP

All of us are inclined to look around and see what our peers are doing and follow their example. When it comes to pensions, this is not a smart approach. If you rely on your pension(s) to deliver your financial expectations when retiring, it's important you recognise the nation's pension habits are woeful, regardless of age group.

As Figure 6 reveals, and Occam observes:

- 75% of employees contribute 5% or less to their pension, regardless of age group.
- Over 50% of employees across all age groups contribute between 3% and 5%.
- Contributing over 7% to your pension would put you in the top 12% of employees across all age groups.

24. If, for example, you received an unexpected bonus or commission you may wish to top up your pension and potentially utilise any unused relief from the previous three years. That would be a smart move. This is an opportunity I refer to as a Moment of Truth (MoT).

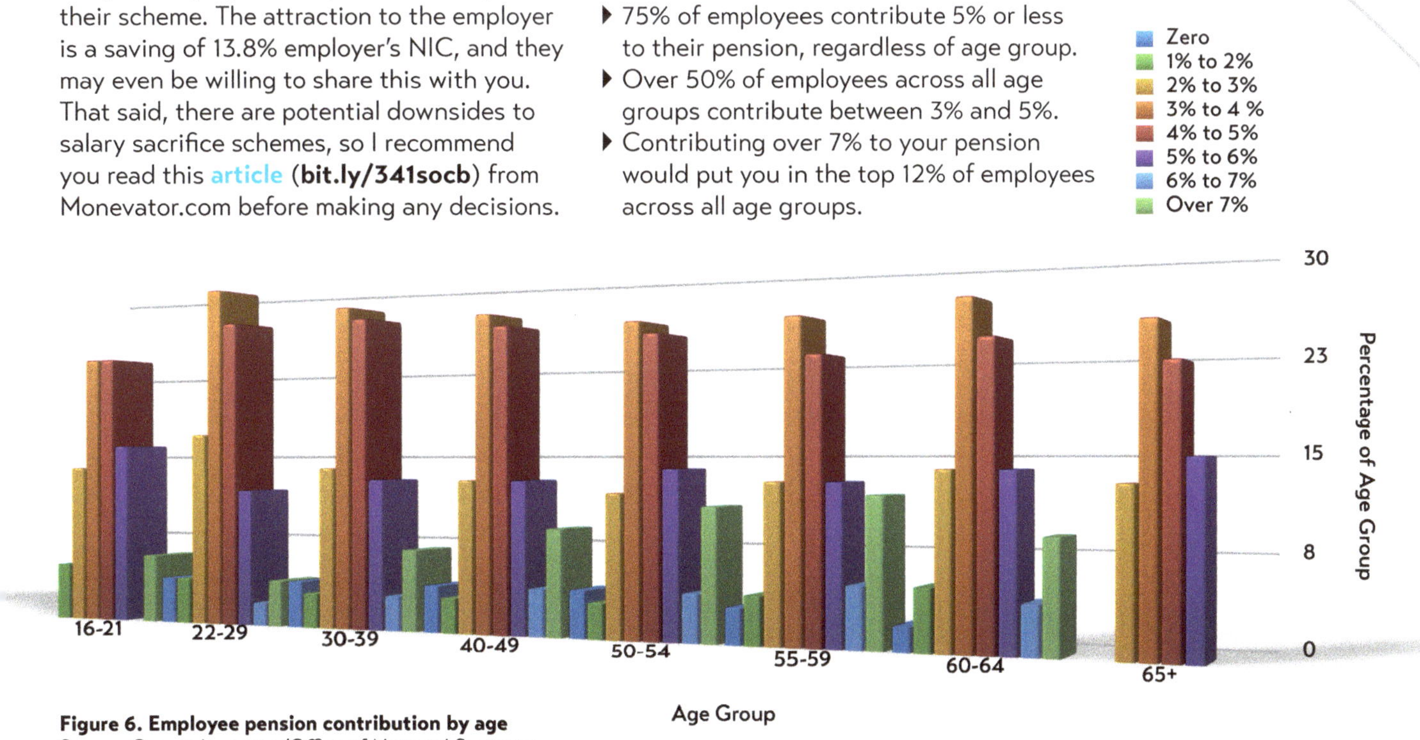

Figure 6. Employee pension contribution by age
Source: Occam Investing/Office of National Statistics

These pension contributions are not impressive, so please don't blindly follow others thinking you'll be okay. You won't.

THE SELF-EMPLOYED AND FREELANCERS

The rules and regulations for the self-employed are basically the same as for everyone else. Though, for obvious reasons, the self-employed have the added burden of taking care of the administration themselves.

In the case of self-employed workers and freelancers, while you will not have an employer pension per se, you can use all your allowances to invest in a SIPP (Self Invested Personal Pension). Most online platforms have one, and are relatively easy to use (see MYFE Book 3). Penfold (**bit.ly/3kWGulp**) is an investment platform tailored for the self-employed and their pension needs. Money to The Masses has a review of Penfold here (**bit.ly/3fmkcZi**).

You can also find a comprehensive and helpful guide to pensions at The Money Advice Service (**bit.ly/2UJvrl6**).

THE GIG ECONOMY AND ZERO-HOUR CONTRACTS

Many Millennials and Generation X live by working several jobs simultaneously in the gig economy. Some by choice, many because there is no viable alternative. In such circumstances, budgeting and planning your finances, especially pension contributions, is difficult, to say the least. There is a blog that may give you some ideas for budgeting at thinkmoney (**bit.ly/3mjeY2I**). The blog's primary advice is to make sure you're claiming all the benefits to which you're entitled, and it has a moderately useful link to that effect.

Just because you work part-time does not mean you're not entitled to an auto-enrolled pension from your employer. If you can, take advantage of it.

If you work for more than one employer, the rules are slightly different. It doesn't mean you're not entitled to auto-enrolment, just that each employer will have to assess whether you should be entered into their scheme. For more information go here (**bit.ly/3kV3LnZ**).

Because you may not be planning to stay long working for certain employers, you might feel it isn't worth the effort (even if you could afford it). You may be right. But the Government has long recognised this problem, and is working to make the 'transportability' of pensions much easier. In the next three to five years it is hoped a 'Pension Dashboard' will be available for everyone to monitor all their pensions in one place. In the meantime, if you need to trace an old pension, go to The Money Advice Service (**bit.ly/3oAzgH0**). A particularly useful website for aggregating all your pension pots is PensionBee. PensionBee does most of the work for you. Remember, every little bit helps.

If you're still uncomfortable investing in a pension that you can't touch until aged 55 (soon to be 57), then whenever you have genuinely spare cash, i.e. cash you know you're not going to need for a few months, place it in a cash ISA. At least that grows tax-free and you can access it tax-free anytime (see page **43**).

Finally, you might want to review some of the blogs hyperlinked on page **81**. There you will find extensive libraries of information and ideas.

WHEN CAN YOU WITHDRAW YOUR PENSION?

The current regulations allow you to withdraw up to 25% of your pension tax-free from the age of 55 onwards.[25] The rules allow you to withdraw this 25% either in one lump sum or in multiple sums over time. Thereafter you can access your pension at any time, but you will be taxed at your marginal rate on any monies you withdraw. The rules and regulations relating to pensions and ISAs outlined in this book are current as of October 2020.

Funds left in your pension pot will continue to grow tax-free.

Aside from perhaps taking a tax-free lump sum at age 55, most people will try to resist accessing their pension pot until they retire. Why? Because if you're still working and earning a salary, your pension 'take' will be added to your income and, most likely, increase your tax liability. It's smarter to wait until you no longer earn a salary, and therefore withdraw from your pension when your tax rate is probably lower. For example, if you have no additional income and take £12,500 from your pension, this would be covered by your personal allowance and would be tax-free.

Under current rules you will only receive the state pension from age 67, at the earliest. The actual date of entitlement will depend on when you were born. Your state pension is added to your earned income for tax purposes.

HEADS UP!

In September 2020, the Government announced plans from 2028 onwards to raise the age at which you can access your pension from 55 to 57. Effectively, that means anyone under the age of 47, or those born after 6th April 1973 (estimated date), needs to plan ahead if they had anticipated accessing their pension at age 55. As of 2028, you will only be able to access a tax-free lump sum or take income from your pension after you reach age 57. A useful explanation can be found at ThisisMoney.co.uk (**bit.ly/3iwYRgp**).

There is another issue of which you need to be aware. Given the large financial debt the Government has acquired during the Coronavirus pandemic, there is every chance taxes will rise to pay for it. If that is the case, the use of tax wrappers will become even more imperative.

NON-EARNERS AND LOW EARNERS

For non-earners and low earners (currently those earning below £12,500), the regulations governing pensions still allow you to invest in one. In these instances, the Government tops up your contribution to the tune of 25%.

As a non/low earner, the maximum you can invest into a pension in any one tax year is £2,880, provided you're under the age of 75. The Government will immediately top this up to £3,600. If you invested £1,000, the top up adds £250. The top-up will be credited directly to your pension.

If you would like to review your pension investment options and see what benefits accrue, a simple but helpful online calculator is available from Hargreaves Lansdown here (**bit.ly/32DY7R5**).

MY EXPERIENCE

It took me a long while to get my head around tax and the various personal allowances. I thought I was being sufficiently responsible and on-the-ball by estimating my tax for the year and then doing the family budget for the following year based on that estimate.

I was always pleasantly surprised when my actual tax was lower than my estimate. What I didn't do, and should have done had I had my wits about me, was take advantage of that opportunity to invest the unexpected 'extra' or 'found' money as a result of paying less tax. This is especially important for those who, like me, didn't start thinking about investments until their forties.

This was one of my Moments of Truth (MoTs), those moments in life when you discover you have more money than you thought from, say, a salary increase, reduced living costs, inheritance, or, as in my case, having to pay less tax. MoTs are the opportunity you need to increase your savings and investments without feeling any pain. I recommend you take advantage of them. They occur more often than you might imagine and can have a significant impact on your future financial wellbeing (see page 23).

The point is: if you've managed to create a saving opportunity for yourself or your family 'bank it.'
Put simply, MOVE IT OR LOSE IT!

SECURE YOUR STATE PENSION

I encourage you to make every effort to secure your full state pension. For most 'workers' this will be done automatically via National Insurance Contributions (NIC) deducted by their employers. But, for those taking extended work breaks, such as parents with small children or those caring for relatives, make sure you claim any automatic credits or consider making voluntary contributions.

To be entitled to a full state pension you need to have made at least 35 years of NIC payments.

25. At some time before age 55 you should consult a financial planner/adviser to review your portfolio of investments just to check you're on track to meet your expectations. If you're not you still have time to do something about it. My recommendation is to pay for such advice on an hourly basis to begin with (average current fee charged is £200 per hour). **Do this before you withdraw any money from your pension.**

REGULATORY RISK

Current regulations allow anyone who dies before the age of 75 to bequeath their pension tax-free to whomsoever they choose. In these circumstances the pension is not only removed from the deceased's estate for Inheritance Tax (IHT) purposes, but beneficiaries may also withdraw any amount(s) tax free. If an individual dies after age 75 then their pension can pass to their beneficiaries free of tax, but those beneficiaries will pay tax at their marginal rate when withdrawing money from the pension.

This book is about financial expectations, so I mention it here simply because it is prudent to remember that all regulations can be changed at a stroke of a parliamentary pen. The freedom to give one's pension tax-free to beneficiaries, or the amount allowable, can be modified at any time.

ISAs

I like pensions, but I like ISAs even more. Why? Because ISAs are more flexible and better in helping us reach our shorter-term financial goals. If 'locking' your savings into a pension is a matter of concern, use ISAs. The beauty of ISAs is their appropriateness for many of your shorter-term financial objectives, including your emergency fund.

As of 2020, you can invest up to £20,000 into a general ISA in any one tax year. The money grows tax-free. You can invest into an ISA at any age, whether or not you have a salary or pension. You can withdraw your money at any time, and unlike pensions, the money you withdraw is not taxed.

One downside of ISAs is that, unlike pensions, you get no tax break on the money you put into them. You will have already paid tax on the money you invest in an ISA and there is no Government top-up on a general ISA.

20% TAXPAYERS WITHOUT EMPLOYER CONTRIBUTIONS

There is an argument stating 20% taxpayers without employer pension contributions would be better off investing in an ISA. The essence of this logic is that for these individuals, upon retiring and drawing down their pension, the Government just takes back their top-up through tax. There is merit to this view, which perhaps accounts for why 50% of the self-employed have no pension (see **Figure 2**).

However, the above approach does not take into account the fact a 20% taxpayer can still withdraw 25% of their pension tax-free. Furthermore, saving in a pension is a form of self-discipline and reduces the impulsive and emotional pressures to dip into ISAs. Lastly, there's no reason, depending on your income and outlook, why you can't proportion your savings between both a pension and an ISA.

LIFETIME ISAs, AND SOME EXTRA CASH

The Lifetime ISA (LISA) is a relatively new tax-free savings and investments wrapper. It is designed to help those who wish to buy their first home.

A LISA is available to, and must be opened by, those aged between 18 and under 40, although only first-time buyers can use a LISA to buy property under age 60. For every £4 you save in a LISA, the Government will add £1 (worth up to £1,000 every tax year until you turn 50 years old). You can save up to £4,000 a year which is eligible for the 25% bonus (you can add more, but it won't receive a Government top-up) until you are aged 50. After you turn 50, the Government will no longer add 25% to your LISA (your money will still be growing and compounding tax-free as is the case with all ISAs).

Your contribution to a LISA forms part of your overall ISA limit of £20,000 pa. Hence, if you invest £4,000 in a LISA one year you can only invest up to a further £16,000 into a general ISA in the same tax year.

You can invest your LISA money into any type of regulated fund.

Remember, you can only withdraw the money before the age of 60 if you use it to buy your first property. After 60, you can withdraw it tax-free whenever you want. If you withdraw your money before 60 and do not use it to buy your first property, you will be hit with a 25% penalty.

You may have heard of Help to Buy ISAs. These, however, are being phased out. From November 2019 it has not been possible to open a new one. Help to Buy ISAs have been superseded by LISAs.

JUNIOR ISAs

Junior ISAs (JISAs) are another form of ISA whereby the money invested grows tax-free. Their beauty lies in the fact that, while they have to be opened by the child's parents or guardian, anyone can contribute to them without affecting their own ISA allowance. Grandparents wishing to contribute towards their grandchildren's education is one example.

The maximum amount that can be placed within a JISA for the 2020/21 tax year is £9,000.

'Junior' cannot access the JISA until they are 18 years of age (there are some exceptions), at which point they alone have access to the funds. It's up to 'junior' entirely if they wish to spend the money on their education, a world tour or a PlayStation.

You can have a cash JISA or a stocks and shares JISA. If the child is 10 or younger, I would recommend a stocks and shares JISA. You can always invest any future contributions into a more secure cash JISA as they approach 18.

MARRIED COUPLES

If you're married to, or in a civil partnership with, someone who has a healthy income, they can transfer money to you completely tax-free, and you can use it to invest in a pension, ISA, LISA or JISA using your own personal allowances.

CALCULATING HOW MUCH AND FOR HOW LONG YOU HAVE TO INVEST

If at any stage you wish to see how much you might have in retirement, or indeed at any time in the future, I suggest you use an online calculator (see Resources, page **83**, for suggestions). Online calculators can help you answer many saving and investment questions. An example can be seen below in Figure 7.

TAKEAWAY

Tax wrappers, be they pensions or ISAs, are available to everyone. Using them helps your money grow faster. Before you place your savings anywhere, think about which tax wrapper you could use.

Financial Calculators & Tools

Want to know how long it might take you grow your savings to a certain size? Use this calculator to get an estimate.

Note: the calculator assumes you have already used your personal savings allowance when selecting a tax rate.

'How Long?' Savings Calculator	
Target sum	£ 150000
Initial lump sum	£ 0
Monthly saving	£ 250
Annual savings interest ?	7 % gross
Are you a taxpayer?	Non-Taxpayer
Annual inflation rate ?	2.5 %
Ignoring inflation, saving your target sum will take	**21 years & 10 months**
After inflation (i.e. in today's terms), saving your target sum will take	**26 years & 5 months**
Reset	Calculate

Assumes a fixed annual return throughout, in practice this will likely vary. Current tax year income tax rates used, these may vary in future, as might savings tax legislation.

Calculations are estimates provided for illustrative purposes only. Candid Money Limited accepts no liability whatsoever for their subsequent use.

Figure 7. How much and for how long will you have to invest in an ISA to meet your financial expectations
Source: Candid Money **(bit.ly/2Szjop6)**

PART **THREE**

Luck is what happens when preparation meets opportunity.

Seneca, Roman philosopher (c. 4BC-65AD)

YOUR NEXT STEP: PLANNING

Every journey requires a plan. Without it you're unlikely to know where you're going or how to get there, to say nothing of why (the 'why' is vital because it's the ultimate motivator). This is true whether you're planning on sailing around the world, or saving for your retirement.

Financial plans are tortuous and intimidating; how can we possibly know what our financial expectations are in 10 years' time, let alone 40? The barrier, therefore, is that the planning process becomes too daunting and we find ourselves paralysed as we realise the uncertainties of our future. You may not be familiar with the old adage 'we plan, God laughs,' but you feel it. As a result many of us adopt what we think is the safer option: 'I don't know what to do, so I'll do nothing.'

What's the solution? The solution is to recognise that your plans and expectations will change over time, it's simply a natural consequence of living. Thus, any plan you develop must be a 'living' plan; that is to say it must be flexible and adapt to your changing needs and whatever life throws at you. In short: when your needs change, change the plan. It really is that simple, although be prepared to take time to implement the change(s). The critical thing is to start your plan today and be prepared to change your plan when life's curveballs come along: bereavement, loss of job, divorce, illness, etc...

You wouldn't plan a road trip without a map. It makes sense, therefore, to create a personal map for your life's financial journey. An excellent book on the subject is The One-Page Financial Plan (**amzn.to/32N09i8**) written by Carl Richards. Additionally, Meaningful Money has a series of short blogs about financial planning, entitled Planning With Purpose, which can be found here (**bit.ly/3rN7oAc**).

Planning requires being organised. With that in mind, I highly recommend the seminal book on the subject, Getting Things Done (**amzn.to/3qjTmGj**) by David Allen. There are many apps to help you prioritise activities and stay organised, my favourite is Things (**bit.ly/3onLmSX**). Things is a task manager structured around the practices identified in David Allen's book. It is unique to Apple hardware, but there are many similar task managers for Windows and Android platforms. To learn how to use Things efficiently I suggest watching Peter Akkies' YouTube video (**bit.ly/3mOZYKN**).

To help with your planning and the priorities you face there is a short 14-point plan located in the Appendix on page **75**, entitled In a Nutshell.

The Things app: Elegant, simple yet powerful, it syncs across all your computers and devices. I used it to help me plan and write all the books in the MYFE series.

Plans are worthless, but planning is everything.

President Dwight D. Eisenhower

IF YOU WANT TO START NOW

If you're motivated to start your financial journey now, but have neither the time nor inclination to read more books, despite lacking the detailed knowledge and confidence to 'go it alone,' there's a solution for that too.

As I have previously mentioned most Independent Financial Advisers (IFAs) have little interest in advising individuals with small amounts to invest, i.e. most Millennials. Additionally, if they do agree to review your financial situation, it'll cost you roughly £1,500+. If you're from Generation X and already have some investments but want guidance at, say, age 55/57 (when you'll finally be able to access 25% of your pension tax-free), you'll still have to pay the £1,500+, but many IFAs will then try to persuade you to let them manage your investments for a further 1% pa (and some will use sophisticated sales techniques to convince you).

Instead consider approaching the following Financial Planners/IFAs/Coaches in whom, having read their offerings, I have confidence:

OPTION 1

Pete Matthew of Meaningful Academy (see page **76**) and Meaningful Money (**bit.ly/2RF3p8M**). Pete not only writes and promotes the 'Meaningful' brand, but is also a partner of Jacksons Wealth Management (**jacksonswealth.com**). Jacksons offers a service for 'New Accumulators,' i.e. those just starting out on their journey. As I understand it, the cost is an initial £500 for a review then £35 plus VAT per month for them to hold your hand and guide you on the details. Provided they have capacity, i.e. they have enough time to bring new clients onboard, I'm sure they'll do you proud.

OPTION 2

Wise Monkey (**bit.ly/3hlOWmO**) is run by Simonne Gnessen, a qualified IFA who decided to shift direction to money mentoring. If you need to first address some poor money habits before you can start saving, Simonne can help you. If you wonder what this service offers read some of the case studies available here (**bit.ly/3c9inxj**). Simonne's focus is to coach people in how to get to grips with their behaviours surrounding money.

Simonne charges £100 per hour and my guess is you'll need at least two to six hours.

Options 1 & 2 enable you to communicate via phone, zoom or in person. The choice is yours.

OPTION 3

The Escape Artist (**bit.ly/2EeKdvm**) website, book and blog written by Barney Whiter is slightly different, and less expensive than options 1 & 2.

Barney is not a qualified IFA, and does not offer specific advice or product recommendations. He is, however, a qualified chartered accountant and worked in the city for 20 years. Barney's coaching service (**bit.ly/3iLWuGM**) will answer your questions via email, phone or zoom.

While Barney, unlike Pete in option 1 above, cannot give regulated investment, tax or legal advice, he is a great sounding board. As he says: "It's about teaching people 'to fish' rather than selling them 'fish.'" The testimonials on the above referenced coaching link speak for themselves.

I have read many of Barney's blogs. They are outstanding; insightful, informative and practical. If you need to run your thoughts by someone because you're not sure which direction to take, or simply want to chew the cud with somebody who understands the issues, Barney's your guy.

MOVING ON

Once you've got a plan, paid off your debt, have an easy access emergency fund and accumulated some savings, the next step is to invest those savings. That's where Books 2 & 3, also available for free at MYFE.guide, will come in handy.

Book 2: How Investment Markets Perform, illustrates why the markets are worthy of your savings. Learning the outcomes of investment market performance over time will help you grasp the basic elements of investing and the various asset classes readily available to you. Moreover, it will help you come to terms with your risk tolerance, while simultaneously giving you some tools to separate the wheat from the chaff. Finally, having a better knowledge of national and international investment markets will give you the confidence to invest, and the mettle to stay the course.

The next step, therefore, is to download MYFE Book 2 and see what it has to say and the guidance it offers.

WHAT MANY PEOPLE DON'T KNOW

Do you know how much your investments have to be worth to provide you with an annual income of £10,000 in retirement?

The answer is at least £300,000 [26] in today's money. Try not to take your 25% tax-free lump sum early.

So, how long will it take to accumulate that amount? Table 8 gives an answer for an ISA.

Now look what happens in Table 9 if your monthly savings are placed in a pension.

UNDERSTANDING TABLE 8 AND TABLE 9

- The tables have been calculated using a constant 7% nominal growth per annum. Thus your effective total real returns are 4.5% in these examples with inflation running at 2.5%. If you keep your investment costs at 0.5%, your annual returns are 4%. Just remember over the next 20 plus years both returns and inflation may go up or down.
- If you're wondering why the individual saving £100 per month in Table 8 shortens their time to target by 15 years in Table 9, while the individual saving £1,000, ten times more, only shortens their time to target by three years, it's because the absolute value of the employer's contribution remains fixed regardless of the amount they saved.
- The numbers have been computed on the basis of 'in today's money,' and thus allow for the inflationary impact of 2.5% every year. This impacts both the saving rate and the final target. For example, saving £1,200 in year one becomes a saving of £1,325 by year five as the starting/saving level is assumed to increase annually with inflation.
- Likewise, the target amount of £300,000 is inflation-indexed in order to be consistent. In this example, and to ensure the purchasing power of your savings remain the same after inflation, the target amount after five years has risen to £331,000.
- Interestingly, after 44 years an individual saving £100 per month (£1,200 per year) with 2.5% annual inflation will have a pension pot of £889,000. But in 44 years' time that pension pot will only generate an income that buys the same amount as £10,000 does today.
- Table 8 assumes these savings have been placed in an ISA, and no tax is paid on the dividends or capital gains. In this instance, therefore, saving £100 per month actually costs £125 of gross income for a 20% taxpayer.
- The pension illustration in Table 9 only assumes basic rate tax relief of 20%. The benefit to higher and additional rate taxpayers is obviously greater.
- Finally, those with employers whose contributions are greater (see example on page **40**) will also reach their monetary target sooner.

26. Your portfolio of investments is unlikely to grow at 3.5% to 4.5% after inflation and costs because during retirement you will need to de-risk your portfolio to hold more fixed income securities, and historically they do not perform as well as shares.

Monthly / Annual Saving	Years to Hit Target
£100 / £1,200	**59**
£250 / £3,000	**40**
£500 / £6,000	**28**
£750 / £9,000	**22**
£1000 / £12,000	**18**

Table 8. How long to save £300k in today's money using an ISA

Calculations based on 7% returns and 2.5% inflation per annum

Monthly / Annual Saving	Annual Pension Top Up	Annual Employer Contribution	Total Annual Savings	Years to Hit Target
£100 / £1,200	£300	£900	£2,400	**44**
£250 / £3,000	£750	£900	£4,650	**32**
£500 / £6,000	£1,500	£900	£8,400	**23**
£750 / £9,000	£2,250	£900	£12,150	**18**
£1000 / £12,000	£3,000	£900	£15,900	**15**

Table 9. How long to save £300k in today's money when using a pension

Calculations are the same as Table 8 but include Government pension top-up with an Employer contribution of 3% for someone earning £30,000 in an auto-enrolled pension

PART **FOUR**

It is better to have a permanent income than to be fascinating.

Oscar Wilde (The Model Millionaire)

QUICK ANSWERS TO FREQUENTLY ASKED QUESTIONS

WHAT'S THE POINT OF INVESTING?

To make your money grow, allowing you to lead a more secure and comfortable life on your terms.

Investing is an efficient way to build wealth. Unlike us, money never sleeps nor does it retire. If invested sensibly it should go on producing capital and creating income long after we put our feet up. Additionally, investing will give you a financial cushion should life throw one of its curveballs at you.

If you leave your money in a bank thinking it's safe, think again. Inflation will steal it.

Had you left £100 in a current bank account in 2002, by 2016 you'd need £149 to buy the same stuff. Put another way, inflation has reduced the value of your money by a third (33%) and your £100 is now only worth £67.

In contrast, had you invested £100 in the FTSE 250 Total Return Index over the same period, your money would be worth £618 in 2016 (before inflation), and £413 (after inflation) – a return of just over 500%.

Inflation easily confuses, mainly because it can be presented in so many different ways. So, look at it this way: after 14 years of inflation (2002 – 2016) what would you rather have, £67 or £413? That's a no-brainer. But unless you do something constructive with your money, you'll end up with the £67.

ITEM	Cost in 2018	Assumed Inflation Rate	Cost in 20 Years	Cost in 40 Years
Postage stamp	65p	2.5%	£1.07	£1.75
Room in nursing home per month	£4,000	3.5%	£7,959	£15,837
Average UK rent per month	£1,017	3.0%	£1,837	£3,317
Getting married	£25,000	4.5%	£60,293	£145,409
Hotel room one night	£140	5.0%	£371	£986
Meal out for two	£50	5.0%	£133	£352

Table 10. Estimated UK inflationary costs of retiring

INFLATION RATE	10 Years	15 Years	25 Years	40 Years
2%	£82	£74	£60	£45
4%	£66	£54	£36	£20
6%	£54	£40	£21	£8
8%	£43	£29	£12	£4
10%	£35	£21	£7	£1

Table 11. How much £100 will be worth in the future given varying inflation rates

Inflation is currently floating at less than 1%. But even at this low level – let alone if it rises – it'll still sting your financial expectations. Most Millennials and many Generation X have become financially aware during a prolonged period of trending low inflation. They (you!) have never experienced its relative cruelty.

At 1% I suspect you will have a tendency to give inflation little thought, let alone consider its impact on your future wealth. Be mindful. Inflation is a killer, and my guess is that it will rear its ugly head again in your lifetimes. Annual average UK inflation in my lifetime stands at 5.3%, and from 1982 to 2015 it averaged 3.6%. Nevertheless, and despite its low current value, its impact on your savings remains pernicious, as Table 11 illustrates.

If inflation soars, you're going to have to work like a dog just to live like one.

George Gobel,
American comedian

The question is: what should you do with your money? Answering that question is the primary purpose of this series of MYFE books.

HOW CAN I START TO SAVE?

There are many ways to save; here are just a few:

- Live within your means. Start by prioritising what's really important to you, and focus on these priorities while sidestepping the nice-to-have items and impulse purchases.
- Learn to budget and manage your income and expenses. Two fabulous, free and downloadable budget planners are available at:

  Martin Lewis's MoneySavingExpert (**bit.ly/2IlkDH4**)
  Pete Matthew's Meaningful Money (**bit.ly/3d9vyPa**)

- For a simple strategic approach to budgeting try this (**bit.ly/34FbceA**). Which? magazine has a useful link for 50 ways to save money (**bit.ly/2FZudye**).
- Budgets can be tiresome, so have a look at 'Dealing with budgets' on page **36**.

If budgets aren't your thing, you might want to read what Jason Butler has to say about an alternative approach here. (bit.ly/3qGqIP5)

One of my favourite anonymous sayings is:

The reason some of us can't save is because of our friends. They're always buying something we can't afford.

By trying to keep up with the Joneses, you're effectively letting someone else determine your life's priorities. Not only is this unsustainable, it's not great for your sense of self-worth either.

If you find yourself tempted to emulate the lifestyles of your friends – and who isn't susceptible to these emotions? – you might like to read The Millionaire Next Door (**amzn.to/2GPYy2z**). It conveys a powerful message and teaches useful habits.

- Learn to acquire the skill of delayed gratification. The famous Stanford marshmallow experiment (**bit.ly/3nmB45B**) established that people who can delay gratification enjoy significantly better life outcomes.
- If you enjoy your day job, give it your best shot. It will improve your chances of promotion and the extra income it brings.
- Start a side-business (as long as it doesn't impact your day job). See the Additional Resources section (page **80**) in this book for ideas.
- Sell stuff you no longer need.
- Use technology to help you save. Money to The Masses quickly reviews a list of potential saving apps here (**bit.ly/3oxo9yA**).
- Read some books on how to save money (see Additional Resources, page **79**). Research the internet for ideas; here's one (**bit.ly/3jyzmev**).
- Watch this video by Jason Butler on How to Get Control of All Your Day to Day Spending (**bit.ly/3gsal38**), or read this blog from MoneySavingExpert (**bit.ly/32ue9fc**).
- Finally, if you're new to the world of managing money and don't know where to start, why not try Damien's Money MOT (**bit.ly/360XNMY**). This will help establish your priorities and guide you on your journey. Damien is the author of the Money to The Masses blog.

Okay, I appreciate the above ideas aren't easy, or even an option for everyone. Nevertheless, for many Millennials and Generation X there are opportunities to save on expenses. Remember, just because you can afford something doesn't mean you should buy it.

WHAT IF I CAN'T SAVE?

Understood. In these circumstances, don't try to save.

Many of us, and for completely genuine reasons, are faced with simply trying to make financial ends meet. The uncertainty of tomorrow's income is too precarious to have the luxury of squirrelling away any savings into pensions or ISAs.

Make the time to visit your local benefits office and make sure you're receiving all the support to which you're properly entitled. When a company I worked for suddenly went bankrupt I was surprised at the financial support I was offered. Even if you think you know the outcome, go anyway; you may be told about a specific benefit to which you will be entitled in the future, especially if your circumstances change.

If you find yourself with spare time, try to make the best use of it. For example, acquire new skills. Assuming you have a computer (if not visit the local library), the government has recently launched a new website at **nationalcareers.service.gov.uk** that may support your efforts in learning new skills, as well as identifying many free online courses.

Going into an office on a Monday morning to be told I was being made redundant with immediate effect was an eye-opener. I even had to wait three months before I got my last month's pay. I was 24 years old at the time. I was lucky, I was able to move back to the family home to live. But the experience did teach me one crucial skill: how to clamp down on expenses and live frugally.

My point is that, doubtless, you too will have learned to live frugally. That is a powerful skill and a major personal strength. Use it. When, hopefully, your situation improves and your income grows and becomes more regular, don't squander your skill of frugality, use it to save more while you can. I know, it's easier said than done, but it's worth it nonetheless.

My experience of redundancy gave me an unexpected professional edge. Having experienced the distress and fear of sudden redundancy, I vowed never to be in that situation again. As soon as I was able, I planned my emergency fund not on the basis of six months' unemployment, but 24. I didn't realise how much unconscious strength this gave me. At work I was always able to speak my mind honestly, knowing if management didn't like it, I was protected by my emergency fund, and besides, I'd faced down redundancy before. The reality was unexpected: I was promoted up the corporate ladder faster than many, and earned a reputation for straight talking and reliability (it's easy to be reliable, and deliver what you promise, if you're honest in the first place).

Minimise your risks; if your income is dependent on a specific piece of kit, e.g. bike/car, mobile or computer, make sure it's insured so you can afford to replace it. That's an investment you have to make, your livelihood depends on it.

There are two vlogs I would encourage you to watch. The first, How to stop living paycheque to paycheque, is by Marko of Whiteboard Finance and is available here (**bit.ly/3k5CzCu**). Marko's vlog gives you an action plan for escaping the paycheque to paycheque trap. The second vlog is by Pete Matthew and entitled The Ultimate Guide to Paying Off Debt (**bit.ly/3mVMIsL**). As the title suggests, if debt is keeping you from saving, Pete's vlog will help. You may also wish to read the section in this book, Debt and your priorities on page **23**.

Living hand to mouth is tough, dispiriting and stressful. There is no magic wand, and too often it feels there's no light at the end of the tunnel. But sometimes there are new opportunities and life skills to acquire. My only advice – and I'm well aware it's inadequate – is to make the most of them when and where you can.

A WORD ABOUT EMERGENCY FUNDS

Most advisers recommend an emergency fund of between three to six months living expenses. However, everyone's situation is different. The best advice I can offer you is to consider how long it will take you to find another job, and plan to fund that period with your rainy-day fund. You might also apply for a part-time job during the interim. The reality is that any amount you can put aside for an emergency is worthwhile, no matter how small.

In my case I was able to find part-time work proofing newsletters, sales brochures and books. Even when I found a new job I carried on with my part-time work which I could do in my own time. Later I lived off my basic salary and saved any commissions/bonuses I received.

I'VE GOT SAVINGS, ISN'T THAT ENOUGH?

No, probably not. Although it does depend on what you mean by 'savings'.

Savings per se are not investments. Savings are invariably cash, and you need to invest your cash in assets that grow faster than inflation. A bank account will not grow faster than inflation.

To make your savings grow you need to invest them.

CAN I INVEST IN MY OWN BUSINESS?

You most certainly can. That said, it's very risky; nearly three out of five businesses fail within the first five years. It isn't that they're bad businesses, many simply just run out of cash (even successful businesses go bankrupt when they expand too quickly without adequate cash resources).

If you start your own business you will work harder than you ever have and endure more anxiety than you thought possible. The upside to managing your own business is that you will be controlling your own destiny and working at your own pace, while feeling a sense of achievement and pride. It clearly isn't an easy path, and it definitely isn't for everyone. For those who succeed it can provide an above average income, especially if, and when, you decide to sell it.

A word of advice: before rushing into setting up your own business, take time to work in your chosen field at an established company to learn the strategic and technical knowledge required to succeed. The experiences will help you establish your own company's unique selling proposition relative to the competition.

Two further advantages of working for another company include:

- It will help you develop your people skills, probably the most important and rewarding skillset any manager needs.
- All managers and entrepreneurs need to be able to prioritise. It's not something they teach you at business school. Working for others may give you an insight into this vital skill.

The Rebel Business School (**bit.ly/3j2v2pp**) may be one free resource to get you going with your own business idea. Due to Coronavirus, events are currently being held online.

CAN'T I JUST GET A FAIR RETURN?

No, not unless you're willing to make an effort to learn the basics of investing.

As a friend of mine once said, in this context:

A fair reward for doing nothing is at best... nothing.

And in case you're wondering, no, constantly switching bank accounts seeking the latest 'loss-leader' interest rate is not a viable long-term strategy. Managing your financial expectations requires making an effort. I'm afraid there's no escaping it.

ISN'T INVESTING A FOOL'S GAME?

No, it isn't. Granted, the investment markets are full of con artists, hucksters and traps for the unwary. Nevertheless, by following a few simple rules, you can make a decent return if you invest over a long enough period and start now. And it will only take half-an-hour of your time once a year.

WHY DON'T I JUST GET A FINANCIAL ADVISER TO DO IT FOR ME?

You could, but it's expensive. UK financial advisers charge around £150 to £250/hr, and most will not conduct a personal investment appraisal for less than £1,500. Furthermore, they may then charge you 1% of your investments every year. On top of that, most financial advisers will not be interested in helping you if you don't have sufficient funds to invest, say, £60,000 or more.

In late 2020 the Financial Conduct Authority (FCA) published a review including an update on how the cost of financial advice has changed following the commission ban at the end of 2012.[27] As expected, it shows financial advisers are generally charging more.

Under the commission system advisers typically earned 3% upfront followed by 0.5% a year. The FCA says the average adviser charge is now 2.4% upfront, i.e. initial assessment and advice, followed by 0.8% a year, with little evidence of reductions for larger portfolios. Whilst a small reduction in initial costs, these will quickly be offset by the significant increase in annual charges.

Many advisers have adopted 1% annual fees, effectively doubling their earnings from the commission days. It is no coincidence another recent survey suggested the average financial adviser now earns around £90,000 a year, compared to £52,000 back in 2012, an increase of 73% (inflation over the same period was 21%).

Some useful links include: 'Financial advisers Tight-Lipped Over Fees' at Which? (**bit.ly/3dYTK7t**). Tip: if an adviser won't tell you their fees over the telephone, just go elsewhere. 'How To Find a Financial adviser' try Which? (**bit.ly/31Gye24**). To learn more about the costs of financial advice visit Which? (**bit.ly/3mpOn5I**).

27. Before 2012 IFAs were paid ongoing commission by the fund managers they selected for your portfolio. This created conflicts of interest insofar as an IFA may select a high commission paying fund that's good for their bottom line but not yours. This practice was therefore stopped through regulation, and is now illegal. The FCA review can be found here (**bit.ly/2Y2a3Jt**), and IFA salary findings are available here (**bit.ly/3o2iY8g**).

ISN'T MY HOME MY PENSION?

If you own enough equity in your home, then yes, it can be. Simply defined, equity is the difference between the market value of your property and the amount you owe on it.

Provided you own enough equity in your home you can borrow against it. Just remember, taking out an equity release loan or a home reversion policy can be expensive. There are many types of home equity release plans available,[28] all with different terms and conditions, so be sure to get professional advice on which one is right for you.[29]

Currently, companies typically limit the amount of cash they will advance to 40% of the value of your equity in the property. The current interest rate of this 'advance' is between 4% to 6%, and at that rate of interest the effects of compounding – and thus your costs – quickly add up.[30] In other words, equity release can be more expensive than obtaining a regular mortgage or loan. Be careful. A helpful explanation can be found at MoneytotheMasses (**bit.ly/3hsCkRX**).

Two things about equity release:

1. If you are in receipt of welfare benefits, acquiring a lump sum through equity release may reduce the benefits to which you're entitled.
2. It's probably a good idea to discuss it with your family before you do it.

Of course, you do have alternatives to equity release or home reversion plans. Here are just five:

- Downsize.
  You may have to move to something much smaller in order to release enough cash for, say, your retirement needs. Alternatively, you may have to move miles away from family and friends to find something suitable. Not great. Either way, it's best to do this while you have your health and energy. Moving homes is stressful and hard work.
- Sell-up and move in with the kids. Good luck with that one.
- Rent your rooms. You can rent rooms in your house up to £7,500 per year tax-free.[31] This option is fine if you've got the space and the temperament.
- Rent a car parking space if you have one. Income from parking spaces is tax-free up to £1,000 per year. Websites exist to help you rent your parking space, try Just Park (**bit.ly/2QkF5IA**).
- Move into something smaller and rent your entire house. But be aware, this will expose you to some of the issues identified in the next FAQ.

None of the above options strike me as a dream come true.

Of course, you could sell the family home while you're still working, but after the kids leave. Be sure to time it right. In the experience of my wife and me, our kids initially kept coming back home – often to our amusement, but always to our delight.

A helpful article on downsizing and the questions to ask yourself can be found at Boring Money (**bit.ly/2J2rFky**). Boring Money is a great website. It's owned and managed by Holly Mackay who does a fabulous job of turning complex questions into clear answers.

Finally, owning your own home is no reason to ignore the investment markets. If you can afford it, invest in both.

28. In 2017 there were 58 schemes. As of August 2019 there were 139 different equity release schemes available to consumers according to the Equity Release Council.

29. A Home Reversion policy is not the same as an Equity Release policy. Please be vigilant.

30. At 5% with no repayments your total debt will double every 15 years.

31. You must personally live in at least 40% of your house to qualify.

ISN'T INVESTING IN BUY-TO-LET (BTL) PROPERTY THE WAY TO GO?

Once again, it can be. Successful BTL requires plenty of homework and hard work. It also has its limitations and risks:

- For BTL landlords the political winds are against you.
- Property is an illiquid asset – you can't sell it quickly.
- The property markets, like the investment markets, suffer from price volatility.
- The tax environment for BTL landlords is becoming increasingly less favourable.

Yes, you can form a company and subsume your property into it, thereby converting the BTL mortgage interest into a deductible expense. However, there are two issues to consider:

1. The process takes time and will incur annual audit fees (this approach is probably therefore more viable for BTL landlords with multiple properties); and
2. Who knows for how long regulations will continue to allow BTL landlords to use this structure to avoid tax on mortgage interest payments?

- Stamp Duty has made the cost of BTL higher and returns lower.
- It is difficult to place your BTL property into a tax wrapper.
- If the property has only ever been rented the BTL landlord will have to pay Capital Gains Tax (CGT) on the difference between the original purchase price and the sale price, the gain (assuming it is sold for more than it was bought). For basic rate taxpayers CGT is 18%, and for higher and additional rate taxpayers the CGT rate is 28%.[32]
- Managing BTL properties is time consuming. It is important to recognise if you invest in the BTL market you are additionally entering a service industry; tenants are entitled to swift and responsive maintenance and repair requests.
- There are numerous costly compliance regulations you will have to meet.
- Finding the right tenants can be expensive; you will have to arrange advertising and credit checks, as well as time consuming (chasing and validating genuine references and interviewing prospective tenants).
- Tenants can become tiresome, to say nothing of troublesome.
- You will have to be prepared to cashflow void periods.
- Many BTL landlords fail to account for all their true costs, e.g. increasing compliance regulations, specialist insurance policies and even CGT, thus giving rise to false income and profitability estimates.
- If you let your BTL property through an agent who is responsible for collecting rents, as well as maintenance and repairs, it is a good policy to speak to your tenants personally at least every six months to assess any problems with the agent's service levels (unhappy tenants are more likely to cause problems).

The secret of profitable BTL investing is, of course, leverage (sometimes called gearing). Even with leverage, however, putting all your money and future financial commitments into one asset class is far from prudent.[33]

Notwithstanding the above comments, during times of high inflation it is considered wise to acquire so-called 'hard' assets. Property is a hard asset.

For a clear, more comprehensive and helpful article on BTL go here (**bit.ly/32s2vS9**) at Woodruff Financial Planning.

32. To establish your personal tax rate please see page **38**.

33. As is the case for most financially leveraged products, you'll need an effective plan for when the music stops, e.g. during economic recessions and pandemics, when tenants have difficulty paying rents. If property leverage is a term you don't understand try watching this video (**bit.ly/36vb0iN**) by Andy Walker. I don't agree with everything Andy has to say. For example, rental income does decline during recessions, especially if you have void periods and need to find new tenants quickly. Furthermore, he avoids mentioning what happens when property prices fall, and you end up owing the bank more than the property is worth, but he does diagrammatically explain the concept of property leverage relatively clearly. For a more balanced view I recommend this video (**bit.ly/3cVlLw9**) with Steve Bolton.

DOES BUYING PROPERTY TO FLIP WORK?

It's worth considering. In this context 'buying property to flip' is the act of buying somewhere with the intention of selling it quickly, frequently after carrying out refurbishments (sometimes called a 'fixer-upper'). Before rushing into such an activity consider the following:

- When undertaking a refurbishment, it is more profitable if you have the skills and time to do much of the work yourself. The higher sale price will justifiably reflect the hard labour you've personally invested, aka 'sweat equity,' and will give you a better return.
- The property market may turn against you while you undertake the refurbishment.
- It's best if you can declare the property as your main residence and thereby avoid Capital Gains Tax on the sale. While there is no official amount of time you have to live somewhere for it to be treated as your home, it is generally considered wise to be there for at least six months to persuade Her Majesty's Revenue & Customs (HMRC) that it is actually your home. It also helps to register to vote at the property and have your post redirected to it. Do not fake your move, HMRC will not be amused.[34]
- Living in a property during refurbishment can put a strain on relationships. After all, not many people want to live in constant chaos. I have a couple of friends who are DIY specialists in their everyday jobs. Ironically it is these very same friends who take forever to complete the refurbishment, and thereby miss profitable sales opportunities. I can only assume by the end of the working week they've had enough DIY. Needless to say, their partners aren't overly impressed.

Please do not misunderstand, I am not saying investing in residential property is a bad idea. It simply isn't a straightforward one. My concern is that I have seen and heard of too many people coming a cropper when they envisage property as a sure-fire way of making money. They assume it's easy and risk-free. It's neither.

My primary focus is to help you make solid long term saving and investment decisions. When reviewing your best options, i.e. those with the highest probability of success and least hassle in terms of meeting your financial expectations, investment markets over time more than meet these criteria.

Those of you interested in the relative performance of property versus other investment asset classes should grab a copy of MYFE Book 2. Book 2 analyses the markets vs BTL, and includes the comparative performance of a hybrid portfolio of BTL investments compared to stock markets.

WON'T I GET RIPPED-OFF IF I INVEST IN THE MARKETS?

You might, which is why you need to spend a little time arming yourself with investment know-how.

AREN'T INVESTMENTS RISKY?

They can be. And yet, just a few simple guidelines will help you avoid foolish and unnecessary risks.

Ultimately, you face two core issues:

- An overarching risk, which is not realising your financial expectations.
- A diminishing opportunity, which is time.

The MYFE series of books will help you overcome both.

By the way, don't let anyone fool you into thinking investment volatility and risk are the same thing. They are not. Volatility is constant and normal; risk is largely a matter of choice.

WHAT DO SMART INVESTORS GET RIGHT?

A number of things:

- They have a plan. It may not be written down or even conscious, but instinctively they know saving and investing is a smart move, so they get on with it.
- They diversify their investments.
- They manage the costs of their investments.
- They appreciate the magic of compounding.[35]
- They use tax wrappers whenever they can.
- They don't panic and sell their investments when markets tumble.
- They don't try to be too clever.
- They have a habit of saving and investing their monthly salary before they spend any of it. This approach is frequently referred to as 'pay yourself first'. The really smart investors do this by setting up monthly automatic direct debits into their saving/investment accounts. Essentially they adhere to the mantra on the next page:

34. HMRC is wise to these behaviours. What is more, if you repeatedly 'buy to flip', you may be deemed to be trading in property. In which case any profits you make will be subject to income tax.

35. Compounding is the inevitable mathematical process whereby you earn interest on the interest you've already earned. It's an exponential calculation, and thus difficult for us to do in our heads. See page **21**.

Do not save what is left after spending. Instead spend what is left after saving.

Warren Buffet, one of the most successful US fund managers in the last 100 years

If you want to explore the ideas behind 'pay yourself first' listen to this podcast featuring Andy Webb of Be Clever with Your Cash and Pete Matthew of Meaningful Academy. It's available here (**bit.ly/33yLR3E**).

There has been much media coverage of late asking why the rich keep getting richer. One answer – though yes, I appreciate there are many other factors at play – is that they follow the aforementioned rules.

WHAT DO BAD INVESTORS DO WRONG?

Several things:

- They start too late.
- They don't bother to acquire basic investment knowledge.
- They pay too much for the management of their investments.
- They take unnecessary risks in an attempt to make up for lost time.
- They are easily swayed by the financial media and chase the latest investment fads.
- They panic and sell their shares when markets head south, thus permanently locking in their losses (rather than waiting for the markets to rebound).

HOW MUCH DO I HAVE TO INVEST?

Many advisers recommend 10 to 15% of your net salary if you wish to maintain the same lifestyle upon retirement. That said, and as usual, opinions differ. Fidelity Fund Management has a helpful article here (**bit.ly/3ef1J09**), which also links to various informative online retirement tools.

But don't be discouraged by that percentage, save as much as you can as soon as you can, even if it's only a small amount. Government pension top-ups, employer pension contributions together with time and compounding will do much of the heavy lifting for you.

Here's a great vlog by Ken Okoroafor (**bit.ly/3o9mloO**) explaining your choices and their consequences when choosing how much you should invest.

EXAMPLE

Assume you and your partner want to retire on £40,000 a year. Also assume you and your partner both retire at age 67, after each making at least 35 years' worth of National Insurance Contributions (NIC). This would currently give you a pension of £9,000 each per annum, that's £18,000 in the bag right there. So, now you need to earn £22,000 per annum from your combined investments. To generate an annual income of £22,000 you'll need a portfolio of £660,000 after inflation. That translates into saving £415 per month between the two of you, or £207 each for 47 years.

Okay, on a gross salary of £20,000 that's potentially a tall order. But it isn't quite the marathon over a mountain you might think. There are two other issues to consider, namely: the above calculation does not take into account the advantages of the government pension top-up, and neither does it include any employer contribution to your pensions.

Revisiting the above assumptions, but now allowing for a government pension top-up for a 20% marginal taxpayer, and an employer pension contribution of 3%, that £207 per month falls to between £100 and £125 of your after tax income.[36] Much less intimidating than you may have supposed.

It's important to recognise that your rate of saving is more important than your rate of investment returns, especially in the early years.[37]

CAN I RETIRE EARLY AND BE FINANCIALLY SECURE?

It's possible. But you may have to work like a Trojan and live like a Spartan to get there.

The FIRE movement (Financial Independence, Retire Early) has gathered momentum in the UK. Its basic philosophy is to earn as much as you can and live as frugally as possible while investing the surplus.

It's an extreme form of lifestyle, but as many followers will tell you, like most habits, such hardships become tolerable, if not easy, over time.

The best-known proponent of FIRE is Mr Money Mustache (**bit.ly/3eHOPtJ**). You may also wish to read the section, A note about FIRE, on page **22**.

36. The £100 to £125 monthly net income difference is dependent on your attitude to volatility during your saving journey. The less you like volatility, the more your monthly contribution should be. The above assumptions are calculated based on 4.5% and 4% annual returns respectively after inflation and costs. By the way, at £100 pm or £1200 pa, this amounts to roughly just a latte a day (£1200 / 365 = £3.28)!

37. Once you've amassed some chunky savings, the rate of investment return becomes more significant – but you still have to keep saving! Here's another interesting and helpful article by Occam Investing (**bit.ly/39sTpsD**).

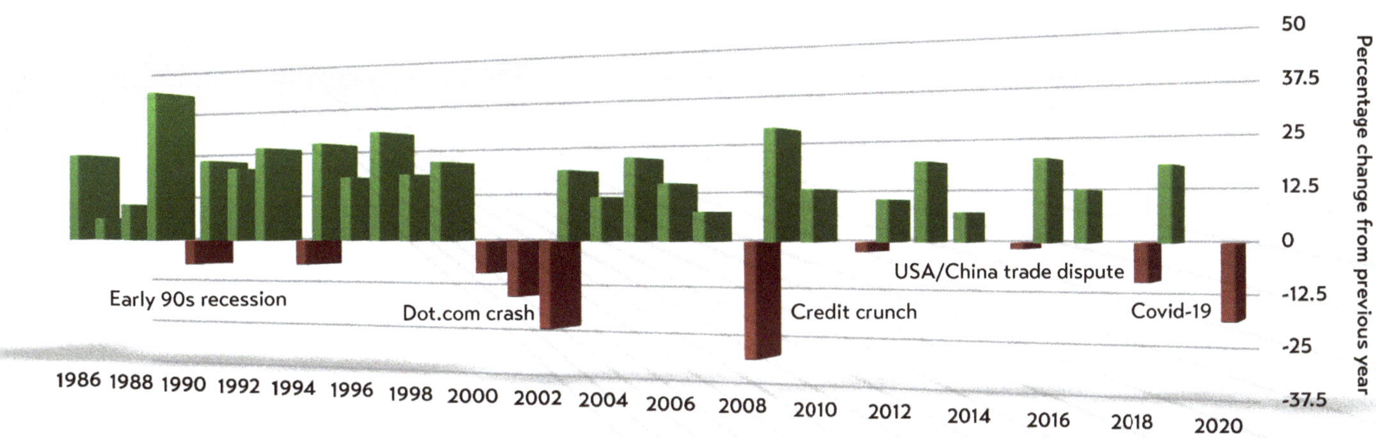

Figure 8. FTSE 100 Total Nominal Returns Index 1985 – 2020 (1st six months only) [38]
Average Returns 8.3% over the period (before inflation and costs)
Source: Refinitiv Datastream

Even if you don't adhere to the FIRE philosophy, with the prospect of many people having to work longer to meet their retirement needs, it's possible to adopt some of the concepts of FIRE to accelerate your saving and investment rate, while simultaneously taking the pressure off having to work so long in retirement. In other words, one notion of the FIRE movement is the idea that you might 'buy' more free time at the end of your working life.

WHERE SHOULD I INVEST?

Start with a pre-packaged diversified fund of index trackers on an inexpensive platform.

If that sounds complicated, don't worry, it's not. Book 2 in the MYFE series, How Investment Markets Perform, explains what a diversified fund of index trackers is, and why they're a smart investment choice. Book 3, Implementing Your Investment Plan, advises you on the how and where to find good funds of index trackers and which platforms to consider. Books 2 & 3 are also available as a free download at MYFE.guide.

HOW FAST WILL MY MONEY GROW?

Historically the markets have delivered an annual long-term return of between 3.5% to 4.5% after inflation and costs.

The good news is that compounding will help your investments grow faster than this level of return instinctively implies.

However, it's important to recognise, and be emotionally prepared for, the fact that annual returns fluctuate, as Figure 8 illustrates (please note these returns are before inflation and costs).

Despite the ups and downs of the FTSE 100, had you invested your savings in the FTSE 100 in 2009 and reinvested the dividends, by 2019 it would have grown 160%. In other words, £100 invested at the end of 2009 would have been worth £260 at the end of 2019 or just over 2½ times your initial investment before inflation and costs.

For a more detailed, yet short, review of your expected returns visit Occam Investment (**bit.ly/2XEtfwD**). While this report sensibly discusses 'real returns', i.e. after inflation, it does not include investment fees and charges.

WHAT'S THE MOST DIFFICULT PART OF INVESTING?

Finding the savings to invest in the first place.

WHAT'S THE ONE SECRET OF INVESTING?

Time. The sooner you start investing, the more your money will grow.

For those of you from Generation X, it may give you some comfort to know I didn't start saving until my forties. Life would have been less trying had I started earlier. What motivated me to get going was an old Chinese proverb:

The best time to plant a tree was 20 years ago. The second best time is now.

Chinese proverb

38. A stock index is a measure of a group of stocks, or a subset of stocks, that helps investors compare current movements in stock values with past values to calculate market performance. Indexes are generally used as a benchmark against which to compare a portfolio of investments. For more details go here (**bit.ly/3weOCqh**).

PART **FIVE**

Your future is created by what you do today. Not tomorrow.

Anon

IN CONCLUSION

Please don't just finish reading this book, hopefully think it's interesting, but then do nothing. I would like to persuade you not to give up before you start. Neglecting to at least start is one of the reasons many people fail to meet their financial expectations. Take action. Stop reading and thinking and start doing! Yes, it's a long journey and you'll have to keep your destination in mind at all times (it will probably change over time, that's natural and okay). The secret is simply this: START NOW. You might also want to take a look at the section, Learning, in the Appendix on page 74.

START NOW

It's not enough to know how to do something, nor is it enough to care. It's only by doing it that you'll make a difference to your world.

The MYFE plan is simple. The biggest secret to its success depends on implementing it now, no matter your age or what stage you're at in your journey.

Even if you can't manage to save 15% of your salary, start small and gradually increase your contributions as opportunities arise.

Providing for your financial future is difficult. At times you will be tempted, or forced, to abandon your journey. If you do, don't beat yourself up, just get back on track as soon as you feel able. Time is your greatest and most critical asset. Alas, it's also non-negotiable. So, please start your investment journey as soon as possible.

FINALLY

Managing your financial expectations is a big ask. And yet, every small step makes a difference. So, as your journey unfolds it may help you to always remember...

Compare yourself to where you were yesterday, not to where someone else is today.

I wish you good luck and good fortune,

Mark

Mark Hamilton

If you think your family, friends or contacts may benefit from this free book, please direct them to the MYFE website (MYFE.guide)

A GOOD CAUSE

Allow me to make the case that a fair amount of effort and expense has gone into making this book freely available to you. If you've found it helpful, then please make a donation to my chosen charity below. Thank you so much – it is truly appreciated!

THE BRAIN TUMOUR CHARITY

Please donate at JustGiving (bit.ly/3xelewo)

APPENDIX

CALCULATING YOUR PENSION CASH COST

Calculating the total amount of your potential pension benefit is not intuitive.

Essentially, an individual's marginal tax rate has no impact on the gross sum that goes into their pension. A net contribution [39] of £1,200 by any individual, regardless of whether they are basic, higher or top rate taxpayers will result in a gross increase in their pension pot of £1,500. Any higher rate relief is given by way of a refund or tax credit, it has zero impact on the size of the pension fund.

The best way to think about your pension contribution from your net salary is in terms of what it actually costs you, your 'cash cost'.

Table 12 and Figure 9 illustrate how it is done.

For example, in the case of a 40% taxpayer the cash cost of making a personal pension contribution of £5,000 is £3,750 (see Figure 9). Firstly, they will receive a government top-up direct into their pension fund of £1,250, giving a gross fund of £6,250. This accounts for the basic rate tax relief. The higher rate relief of a further £1,250 is given by way of a tax reduction. Hence the actual cash cost of £3,750.

For those who are employed the higher rate relief is usually given through the PAYE system. For self-employed workers and freelancers the relief is claimed as a reduction in their personal tax bill. In either case it is important the individual makes a claim for the additional relief either through their Self Assessment tax return or direct to HMRC.

39. Your net contribution is the amount you pay in after tax has been deducted from your salary.

A useful calculator for estimating your pension in retirement can be found here. (bit.ly/3uocMLm)

Annual Net Contribution	Basic Rate Government Top-Up	Gross Pension Contribution	Your Marginal Tax Rate	Additional Tax Relief Due	Actual Cash Cost of Contribution
A				B	(A - B)
£1,200	£300	£1,500	20%	**£0**	**£1,200**
£1,200	£300	£1,500	40%	**£(300)**	**£900**
£1,200	£300	£1,500	45%	**£(375)**	**£825**

Table 12. Example of the pension benefit

$$\text{Your cash cost} = (£X^* \div 0.8) - (£X^* \div 0.8 \times \text{'your marginal tax rate'})$$

Figure 9. Calculating your actual cash cost

*** X is your annual net contribution**

I constantly see people rise in life who are not the smartest, sometimes not even the most diligent, but they are learning machines. They go to bed every night a little wiser than they were when they got up and boy does that help, particularly when you have a long run ahead of you.

Charles Munger, Vice Chairman of Berkshire Hathaway, renowned investment manager and philanthropist

So, where does this tax credit/refund come from? It is the amount of tax the government would have taken from you had you not invested in your pension. In the 40% taxpayer example opposite, the amount of tax saved is £1,250.

Those on the basic tax rate need do nothing more. If, however, you are on higher or additional tax rates you have a decision to make: what are you going to do with the 'saving' or 'found money' from this cash cost? You can spend it or you can invest it elsewhere, e.g. in an ISA. You already know the answer: **MOVE IT OR LOSE IT!**[40]

Your rate of savings, especially initially, is more important than your investment returns when it comes to meeting your financial expectations. The reality is many people are blissfully unaware of this 'saving', and just spend it.

CALCULATING YOUR INVESTMENT RETURNS

In the context of the MYFE series of books your Rate of Return (RoR) and Return on Investment (RoI) are used interchangeably.

Both measures establish the net gain or loss of an investment over a specified time period, expressed as a percentage of the investment's initial cost. When calculating the rate of return, you are determining the percentage change from the beginning of the period until the end.

Both metrics can be used on a variety of assets: from stocks to bonds or real estate to gold. They measure how well, or not, your investment has performed over and above your initial capital outlay. For example if the RoR is 100% then your money has doubled in value; you've turned your £100 initial outlay into £200. If your RoR is 125%, you've turned your invested capital from £100 to £225.

The formula for calculating your RoR is:

Rate of Return = (Final Asset Value – Initial Asset Value) ÷ Initial Asset Value[41]

The effects of inflation are not taken into consideration in this simple rate of return calculation, but would be if you were comparing real rates of return.

If you use the formula to compare two investment returns, make sure you measure them over the same time period.

40. You can invest this extra cash in a SIPP and receive an additional Government top-up (provided you have not exceeded your pension allowance – see page **41**), or an ISA.

41. Your initial Asset Value is the price you paid when you invested in the asset at the beginning of the time period.

PAYING OFF DEBT

A useful spreadsheet for calculating how best to pay off your debt is available as a free download from Vertex42 (**bit.ly/3k1xCdJ**). Its primary purpose is to show the difference between the snowball and avalanche methods. However, Figure 10 and Figure 11 illustrate a number of other significant variables. For example, the date at which you will pay off a debt and the implications of how much each month you decide to allocate towards those various debts.

WHAT YOU'RE LOOKING AT

In Figures 10 and 11, the spreadsheets compare the implications of paying off your debt with the minimum payments necessary, either via the snowball (smallest debt first) or the avalanche (highest interest first) method.

Note that by following the snowball method you will pay £76,683 interest on your loans and will finish paying off all your debt in 27 years (assuming you began paying down the debt on 1/06/21). Following the avalanche method you will pay £64,391 in interest (a saving of £12,292) and finish in 24 years.

WHAT HAPPENS IF YOU INCREASE YOUR DEBT PAYMENTS?

Staying with the avalanche method, but increasing your monthly contribution by £200 towards your debt payments, the spreadsheet in Figure 12 shows you the outcomes. The additional £200 per month reduces the amount of interest you will have paid on your debt to £13,270 and you will have paid off all your debts in 7½ years.

By the way, if you look around the Vertex42 (**bit.ly/36cMFN5**) website you'll find many other free Excel templates of potential value. There are video resources to learn how to use the spreadsheets here (**bit.ly/2U4VhPW**).

As with many aspects of financial planning, there is no single 'correct' answer for everyone. There are many advisers who advocate paying off all your debt as soon as possible, even if it means you have no emergency fund. Their argument is that if you have small and manageable debts you will be able to borrow from your bank in times of emergency or seeking a mortgage. Thus an emergency fund is not vital, meanwhile you save money by paying off your debts early. A valid point, but not, in my view, always compelling.

Debt Reduction Calculator vertex42

https://www.vertex42.com/Calculators/debt-reduction-calculator.html © 2007-2020 Vertex42 LLC

Balance Date: 01/06/2021

Creditor Information Table

Row	Creditor	Balance	Rate	Payment	Custom	Interest-only
1	Card #1	£4,400	21.00%	£80	2	77.00
2	Auto Loan #1	£3,200	9.81%	£27	1	26.16
3	Auto Loan #2	£5,000	12.00%	£50	3	50.00
4	Card #2	£9,000	18.00%	£135	5	135.00
5	Student Loan #1	£15,500	4.00%	£55	4	51.67
6						-
7						-
8						-
9						-
10						-
	Total:	37,100.00		347.00		

Monthly Payment: 350.00
Initial Snowball: 3.00

Strategy: Snowball (Lowest Balance First) Choose a strategy

Creditors in Chosen Order	Original Balance	Interest Paid	Months to Pay Off	Month Paid Off
Auto Loan #1	3,200.00	4,048.33	204	Jun-2038
Card #1	4,400.00	10,740.90	190	Apr-2037
Auto Loan #2	5,000.00	11,201.85	242	Aug-2041
Card #2	9,000.00	35,683.46	283	Jan-2045
Student Loan #1	15,500.00	15,008.88	326	Aug-2048
	-	-	-	
	-	-	-	
	-	-	-	
	-	-	-	
	-	-	-	

Total Interest Paid: **76,683.42** Debt Free: **Aug-2048**

Results are only estimates

Figure 10. Snowball method

Debt Reduction Calculator vertex42

https://www.vertex42.com/Calculators/debt-reduction-calculator.html © 2007-2020 Vertex42 LLC

Balance Date: 01/06/2021

Creditor Information Table

Row	Creditor	Balance	Rate	Payment	Custom	Interest-only
1	Card #1	£4,400	21.00%	£80	2	77.00
2	Auto Loan #1	£3,200	9.81%	£27	1	26.16
3	Auto Loan #2	£5,000	12.00%	£50	3	50.00
4	Card #2	£9,000	18.00%	£135	5	135.00
5	Student Loan #1	£15,500	4.00%	£55	4	51.67
6						-
7						-
8						-
9						-
10						-
	Total:	37,100.00		347.00		

Monthly Payment: 350.00
Initial Snowball: 3.00

Strategy: Avalanche (Highest Interest First) ← Choose a strategy

Creditors in Chosen Order	Original Balance	Interest Paid	Months to Pay Off	Month Paid Off
Card #1	4,400.00	8,168.93	152	Feb-2034
Card #2	9,000.00	25,582.59	217	Jul-2039
Auto Loan #2	5,000.00	11,375.97	238	Apr-2041
Auto Loan #1	3,200.00	5,904.48	247	Jan-2042
Student Loan #1	15,500.00	13,359.45	290	Aug-2045
	-	-	-	
	-	-	-	
	-	-	-	
	-	-	-	
	-	-	-	

Total Interest Paid: **64,391.42** Debt Free: **Aug-2045**

Results are only estimates

Figure 11. Avalanche method

My reasons are fivefold:

1. Some long-term debt, such as a mortgage, becomes increasingly less onerous with the passing of time and the impact of inflation. Provided your salary keeps roughly in-line with inflation (and most people's do), the relative size of your mortgage declines.
2. An emergency fund offers peace of mind.
3. Investing additional savings, instead of just applying them to pay off your mortgage early, introduces you to the markets and allows you to benefit from the knowledge and experience.
4. Having a combination of savings, emergency funds and investments, as opposed to just having a smaller mortgage, gives you more options should circumstances change.
5. Banks have their own priorities, you cannot rely on them. You may be able to take out a loan from your bank if and when the need arises, but, then again, given the prevailing economic environment, that loan might be very expensive indeed. And that assumes you can get a loan in the first place.

Many aspects of financial planning are not black and white, but on balance, the more flexibility you have when facing the uncertainties of life, the better.

Debt Reduction Calculator

vertex42

https://www.vertex42.com/Calculators/debt-reduction-calculator.html

© 2007-2020 Vertex42 LLC

Balance Date: 01/06/2021

Creditor Information Table

Row	Creditor	Balance	Rate	Payment	Custom	*Interest-only*
1	Card #1	£4,400	21.00%	£80	2	77.00
2	Auto Loan #1	£3,200	9.81%	£27	1	26.16
3	Auto Loan #2	£5,000	12.00%	£50	3	50.00
4	Card #2	£9,000	18.00%	£135	5	135.00
5	Student Loan #1	£15,500	4.00%	£55	4	51.67
6						-
7						-
8						-
9						-
10						-
	Total:	37,100.00		347.00		

Monthly Payment: 550.00
Initial Snowball: 203.00

Strategy: Avalanche (Highest Interest First) ← Choose a strategy

Creditors in Chosen Order	Original Balance	Interest Paid	Months to Pay Off	Month Paid Off
Card #1	4,400.00	780.89	19	Jan-2023
Card #2	9,000.00	4,421.87	45	Mar-2025
Auto Loan #2	5,000.00	2,539.09	56	Feb-2026
Auto Loan #1	3,200.00	1,546.85	63	Sep-2026
Student Loan #1	15,500.00	3,981.33	92	Feb-2029
	-	-	-	
	-	-	-	
	-	-	-	
	-	-	-	
	-	-	-	

Total Interest Paid: **13,270.03** Debt Free: **Feb-2029**

Results are only estimates

Figure 12. Increasing debt payments by £200

MANAGING STUDENT DEBT

Before offering my own narrative on student debt, it's important you should know that the maestro on the subject is Martin Lewis of the Money Saving Expert blog. Martin has produced at least two blogs on the subject, available here (**bit.ly/2IJQCRA**) and here (**bit.ly/2IKwsH5**). Martin has created an outstanding written guide, and also a compelling vlog – I highly recommend them. In fact, if you're grappling with, or simply worried about, the issue of student debt, I would say they are compulsory reading/viewing!

My own example overleaf covers those student debts incurred on or after 1st September 2012. This therefore only relates to some Millennials, but no one from Generation X (unless you're a parent of a university student). I have chosen to do this because I assume those of you from Generation X have already addressed the issue. That said, please note some rules have been changed retrospectively, and may therefore need revisiting. Martin's first blog has a video aimed at those who acquired their debt before 2012. In general, for Generation X the answer to whether you should pay off your student debt early is no.

A bank is a place where they lend you an umbrella in fair weather and ask for it back when it begins to rain.

Robert Frost, American poet

If you started an undergraduate course on or after 1st September 2012 you will be obliged to start repaying your loans once your gross salary, i.e. your income before tax, reaches £26,575 per year (see below if you started before 1/9/12).

The following are cut and pasted extracts from Gov.uk (**bit.ly/35y7d3p**). For example:

PLAN 1

**[if you started an undergraduate course before 1/9/12]
The thresholds are £372 a week or £1,615 a month (before tax and other deductions).**

EXAMPLE
**You're paid monthly and your income changes each month. This month your income was £2,000, which is over the Plan 1 monthly threshold of £1,615.
Your income was £385 over the threshold (£2,000 minus £1,615). You will pay back £34 (9% of £385) this month.**

EXAMPLE
**Your annual income is £27,000 and you're paid a regular monthly wage. This means that each month your income is £2,250 (£27,000 divided by 12). This is over the Plan 1 monthly threshold of £1,615.
Your income is £635 over the threshold (£2,250 minus £1,615). You will pay back £57 (9% of £635) each month.**

PLAN 2

**[if you started an undergraduate course on or after 1/9/12]
The thresholds are £511 a week or £2,214 a month (before tax and other deductions). They change on 6 April every year.**

EXAMPLE
**You're paid weekly and your income changes each week. This week your income was £600, which is over the Plan 2 weekly threshold of £511.
Your income was £89 over the threshold (£600 minus £511). You will pay back £8 (9% of £89) this week.**

EXAMPLE
**Your annual income is £28,800 and you are paid a regular monthly wage. This means that each month your income is £2,400 (£28,800 divided by 12). This is over the Plan 2 monthly threshold of £2,214.
Your income is £186 over the threshold (£2,400 minus £2,214). You will pay back £16 (9% of £186) each month.
[If you have a postgraduate loan your numbers, and therefore your payback mechanisms, are different again. The above link will give you details.]**

You have no choice in the matter, you have to pay these amounts.

The tricky bit comes in deciding whether or not to accelerate paying off your student debt. There is no penalty for doing so.

Table 13 gives the current rate (as at March 2020) of interest charged on your student debt. Thus the total interest is an RPI of 2.6% plus 3% = 5.6% (but only for those earning above £26,576). 5.6% is not an astronomical rate, and, if inflation falls, may even decrease over the coming months – although don't count on it!

The question is: if, after you've repaid all high-interest debt and maxed-out your employer's pension contribution and have an emergency fund, and you still have spare savings or have acquired a lump sum, what should you do with them? Put them towards paying off your student debt, allocate them to an ISA money fund for something you're hoping to acquire in the next five years, e.g. a property deposit, or invest for the long-term?

If you're thinking about investing for the long-term, it will help you to compare your student debt interest to your expected long-term stock market returns. This, however, raises another question: what stock market returns should you be comparing your 5.6% student interest against? Total real returns or total nominal returns?

HOW YOU MIGHT APPROACH YOUR DECISION – A GUIDE ONLY

Though I have previously stated total real returns are the ones that matter most to you over the long haul, in this context I would recommend making the comparison against total nominal returns. Why? Because you are then comparing like with like. However, keep a watchful eye on inflation since this will impact the rate at which you payback your student debt, and could swiftly change the balance of outcomes.

So, what equity returns can you expect? It's a judgement call, but **Figure 8** shows the FTSE 100 has delivered an average nominal total returns of 8.3% over the last 12 years. As you will discover in MYFE Book 2, that's quite a strong performance. Accordingly, I would be inclined to row-back a little on that benchmark and guess at somewhere between 6%–7%, still better than 5.6%. Of course, you will have to deduct your investment costs, but as you will see in MYFE Book 3, these can be kept to less than 0.5%.

Please recognise that in offering this approach I am sticking my head above the parapet. Others may well disagree, and strongly, with good reason. Making such determinations is not easy and fraught with unknowns and caveats. In suggesting this strategy I am fundamentally demonstrating the need to approach such matters rationally, rather than emotionally.

Your Annual Income	Interest Rate
£26,575 or less	RPI (currently 2.6%)
£26,575 to £47,835	RPI (currently 2.6%) plus up to 3%
Over £47,835	RPI (currently 2.6%) plus 3%

Table 13. Student Loan Interest

PARENTS WANTING TO HELP

Many parents are aghast at the prospect of their children ending their university education with a debt of, say, £40,000 to £60,000. In their desire to help they either personally fund their child's tuition fees and costs (so there is no debt at the end), or they pay off the debt as soon as they can.

Do not be too hasty. The student loan scheme is more generous and forgiving than you might suppose.

Students may never have to pay off the debt. Even if they do, under current regulations they will only pay 9% of their salary above £26,575 towards the debt. Furthermore, if after 30 years from completing their higher education the debt has not been fully paid off, the slate is wiped clean.

I appreciate this is very much a personal, ethical and emotional issue, not just financial. Nevertheless, parents might want to hesitate paying off their children's higher education loans, preferring instead to sit down with them and explain that a better option might be to spend the £40-60k by way of a house deposit rather than repayment of student debt. To be frank, depending on their work and income profiles over the next three decades, there is a very real possibility their children will not earn sufficient to make a material dent in their student debt by the time it is written off in 30 years. If you have the money to give them now, why not give it to them to invest in an ISA. At the very least, let the money grow in your own investment accounts until such time as you are prepared to pass it on.

With those caveats in mind, it is worth noting if a child is in full-time education or under the age of 18, parents can pay for rent, tuition fees and maintenance without there being any Inheritance Tax (IHT) implications.

- To cover the child's rent a parent can pay the landlord or agency by direct debit or standing order.
- Tuition fees can be paid direct to the university.
- A parent can transfer money into their child's account for general living expenses on a monthly basis.

Once again, allow me to stress how helpful Martin Lewis's online blogs/vlogs are. They will clarify so much for you.

There is no set limit for maintenance money. However, it needs to be considered a reasonable sum to cover things like food, bills and spending money. If it is excessive, Her Majesty's Revenue & Customs (HMRC) may deem there is a 'gift' element, and this could have IHT implications. The issue of IHT will only arise in the event of a death of a parent within seven years. Even then, the contributions will almost certainly be covered by one or more reliefs and exemptions such as 'family maintenance', 'gifts out of income' or the normal annual inheritance tax allowance.

LEARNING

Like many people, I prefer to set aside some clear space and time when planning to learn a new subject or tackle a tricky issue about which I need to be better informed.

The challenge, of course, is finding that space and time. Somehow it's never there. The everyday business of life commands our constant attention and energy. Result: we never get around to doing the things we should, even those things we know are important. Coincidentally, this is one of the main reasons so many people fail to meet their financial expectations.

I also feared the learning I had to do would require concentrated, and potentially painful, effort. Yet another reason to avoid getting on with it!

The other deception we practise is in convincing ourselves we're actually doing something constructive by collecting bits and pieces (newspaper cuttings, books, articles, blogs, etc...) about the subject we plan to study, and then neatly filing them away for some future review. The truth, of course, is that we're simply building a mountain for ourselves to climb – requiring yet more space and more time. And the bigger the task becomes the less we want to confront it.

Finally I came to realise I didn't need so much space and time to get started with the process of learning.

All I needed was to have my brain in gear (but definitely not in overdrive), and 10 to 20 spare minutes. I began to read and investigate stuff I needed to know, but I did not apply any pressure on myself to make decisions. In other words, I chose to make a series of small steps rather than one giant leap. I didn't even pressure myself to understand every element of what I was reading. I was just 'feeling' it.

Slowly but very surely I made progress. What's more, without any additional effort at all – i.e. without the need to ring-fence valuable space and time – I allowed myself to quietly absorb what I had read (even if I didn't fully understand it), as if by osmosis. Result: not only did I come out the other end sooner, I was far better informed than if I had attempted to achieve everything in one monster learning session.

At the start of this book there are two quotations. One by the Chinese philosopher, Laozi, the other by Barack Obama. Both acknowledge the need to start the journey now and gradually.

The point is: learning necessitates making a series of small steps, and everyone of those steps gets you nearer to where you want to go – no matter the distance. All you have to do is be willing to start now!

IN A NUTSHELL

Achieving financial independence requires effort. Without a sense of direction it's nigh impossible. Knowing where you're going is halfway to getting there. MYFE is therefore designed to help you create a plan to achieve your financial goals. Below is a specific 14-point road map around which MYFE is structured. Don't worry if some elements of the plan make little sense now, they will soon.

1 Create a financial plan. Take time to establish your individual financial goals and their respective timeframes.

2 Undertake a domestic budget exercise to determine how much you can save/spend.

3 Be sure to consider what insurance protection you may need, and include the premiums in your budget.

4 If you have a company pension, try to maximise your employer's match.

5 Pay down your debt – especially credit card debt – but not necessarily your mortgage.

6 Establish an easy access emergency fund.

7 Learn to save. Prioritise and think about saving opportunities, use technology to help you identify those moments and develop financial discipline.

8 Decide how much of your savings to allocate to each of your financial goals. Saving for a home and your retirement fund are your highest priorities.

9 Determine which, if any, tax wrapper is appropriate for each of your financial goals. The tax rules are more generous than you might think.

10 Understand the tried and tested principles of sound investment strategies. Don't try to be too clever.

11 Select the route for investing in the markets that is best for you. Do not use the same company or platform as your partner.

12 Take a snapshot of your net worth every year to help keep you on track. Measure your investment returns against independent indexes at least every three years.

13 Make a will. Do not let those you care for, or those for whom you are responsible, suffer the additional delay and anguish of you dying intestate.

14 Do it ASAP. The most powerful tool available to investors is time. Time is your single greatest ally on the road to financial independence, and it's free! But it's also non-negotiable and irreplaceable, so please make the most of it.

While the plan is relatively simple, achieving it won't be. There will be times when you will have to put your investment journey to one side. That's okay, it happens to us all. Just try to get back on track as soon as possible. Remember, if you make the effort now your future self will thank you – big time!

ADDITIONAL RESOURCES

I have only felt confident enough to write the MYFE books because generous authors have shared their market knowledge and investment experiences through books, websites and blogs.

I include below some of those I consider worth reading at this stage of your journey. You may also prefer to learn about financial planning through a blended approach, i.e. books, blogs, videos, podcasts. These additional resources offer you that choice.

SPECIAL MENTIONS

Meaningful Money
Meaningful Academy
THE MEANINGFUL MONEY HANDBOOK
by Pete Matthew

I came across Pete Matthew's book late in my research. I was sufficiently impressed to extend my research into the other activities Pete undertakes. What I discovered is the greatest body of financial advice for UK savers and investors. It is a truly amazing trove by a qualified financial planner who understands their topic, their market and delivers that extensive knowledge engagingly. If you go anywhere to improve your understanding of how to meet your financial expectations go to Pete. You will not regret it.

The 'Meaningful' brand has podcasts, blogs, videos, and a unique academy of courses. So taken was I by Pete's offerings I decided to subscribe to his Meaningful Academy Courses. They aren't the cheapest I've come across, but they are the best and worth every penny. Pete has also launched a unique series of free podcasts entitled the Millennial Challenge; these can be accessed here **(bit.ly/2Se7xg6)**.

Truth is, had I discovered Pete's wonderful treasure chest of financial guidance, I might have been tempted simply to have paid for my kids to subscribe to his various courses instead of writing MYFE! Pete has written a fabulous booklet especially for Millennials which can be downloaded here **(bit.ly/34G51VI)**.

Coincidentally, Meaningful Money is supported and sponsored by Seven Investment Management. 7iM was co-founded by Justin Urquhart Stewart. Many moons ago I heard Justin on the radio, and not knowing where else to turn, as a twenty-something I cold-called him. Justin graciously took my call and generously answered my questions. Not once did he make me feel my questions were dumb. I have never forgotten his kindness, and it comes as no surprise to me that Justin continues to value 'spreading the knowledge' by supporting the output of the Meaningful brand. Thank you, Justin, from all of us.

REGIONALLY
GROWING INVESTMENT

Recently launched, Regionally.com, is a new investment concept launched by Justin Urquhart Stewart. Its aim is to support communities by allowing retail investors to select specific companies in their region into which they can invest their savings. At the same time, local companies can apply to Regionally to become one of the selected businesses wishing to raise working capital.

Unlike Peer-to-Peer (P2P) lending platforms, Regionally applies a more rigorous approval process when vetting companies seeking investors, and, in 2021, will develop a secondary market for equity, debt and convertible loans for investor members to buy/sell shares and bonds. Moreover, Regionally conduct on-going monitoring of each company's performance post-investment.

Not surprisingly, Justin and his colleagues have found another original way to further help communities, their businesses and retail investors.

I'm not suggesting as a beginner that you invest in individual companies. But if you belong to Generation X, and already have substantial funds, you may want to investigate Regionally for an investment in your neck of the woods.

MY FAVOURITE BLOGS

During the past five years of research I have come across hundreds of saving and investment websites and blogs. Here are three of my favourites:

Occam Investing

Occam Investing (**occaminvesting.co.uk**) is a true exception amongst the financial blogosphere. Occam is an independent blog written by someone who works in the fund management business but has no axe to grind, and isn't interested in selling you anything – except great advice. Aimed at both new and experienced investors, it is clearly written and analyses core saving and investment issues. Even if you're new to investing you'll understand the content. What's different about Occam is that it uses reliable data, and thoughtfully presents its messages using telling infographics. Outstanding!

Monevator

Monevator (**monevator.com**) is another of my personal 'go-to' websites and blogs on most investment topics. It is intended more for the intermediate investor who already has some knowledge. Nevertheless, the library of articles and topics is so extensive that should you have any issues or questions you will doubtless find some informative and constructive thoughts here. What's more, the blog is written in a wonderfully accessible style with great humour.

THE ESCAPE ARTIST

I have already referred to the value of The Escape Artist (see page **50**). This is a first class website/blog. Barney, the author, has a unique narrative when introducing key saving and investing concepts which may resonate with you (it certainly does with me) and, more importantly, helps you understand and remember the core skills for planning your financial future. I always look forward to his weekly email newsletters.

BOOKS

YOUR MONEY MATTERS

by Martin Lewis

If you are a complete beginner to finance with little understanding of the terminology, let alone the methodology, Martin's book is for you. It's clearly written and beautifully illustrated, and it's free to download. There's also a Teacher's Guide to go with it, and that too is free to download. Your Money Matters has been designed for use by young people and covers topics including:

Saving and spending • Borrowing • Good and bad debt • Risk and reward Insurance • Investments • Future planning around student loans • Tax and national insurance.

TOTAL MONEY MAKEOVER

by Dave Ramsey

I haven't read this book, but with 4½ stars from 6,153 reviews it's clearly worth consideration. The focus of the book is helping you get out of money problems, i.e. debt, and back on track. It's written for the USA market, but from what I can tell it offers advice to anyone in financial difficulty. Here's the sales blurb, and it's very American, but don't let that deter you:

"Build up your money muscles with America's favourite finance coach. Okay, folks, do you want to turn those fat and flabby expenses into a well-toned budget? Do you want to transform your sad and skinny little bank account into a bulked-up cash machine? Then get with the program, people. There's one sure way to whip your finances into shape, and that's with The Total Money Makeover: Classic Edition. By now, you've heard all the nutty get-rich-quick schemes, the fiscal diet fads that leave you with a lot of kooky ideas but not a penny in your pocket. Hey, if you're tired of the lies and sick of the false promises, take a look at this book. It's the simplest, most straightforward game plan for completely making over your money habits. And it's based on results, not pie-in-the-sky fantasies. With The Total Money Makeover: Classic Edition, you'll be able to: Design a sure-fire plan for paying off all debt, meaning cars, houses, everything. Recognise the 10 most dangerous money myths (these will kill you). Secure a big, fat nest egg for emergencies and retirement!"

BOOKS TO HELP YOU GET STARTED

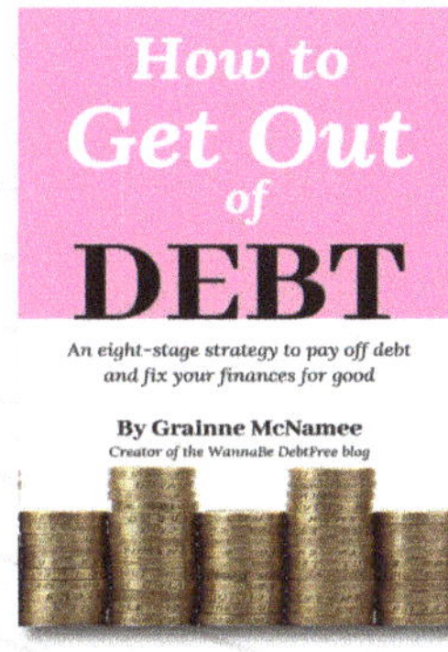

THE MILLIONAIRE NEXT DOOR

by Thomas Stanley & William Danko

This book is both a treat and a revelation. By studying citizens from across America, Professors Stanley and Danko reveal how the average millionaire is not interested in flashy displays of wealth. Indeed, quite the opposite. The book delves into the philosophies and purchasing patterns of those who have slowly and quietly acquired a financially comfortable life. For those of us who think we've 'arrived' once the BMW is parked outside, think again. This book shows us why, and what to do about it.

GIVE & TAKE (amzn.to/2Z7hGyO)

by Adam Grant

This is an upbeat read, essentially conveying why nice guys can finish first. It's a testament to committing and making an effort to do your best in both professional and social relationships. Here's just one of many reviews:

"In this riveting and sparkling book, Adam Grant turns the conventional wisdom upside down about what it takes to win and get ahead. With page-turning stories and compelling studies, Give & Take reveals the surprising forces behind success and the steps we can take to enhance our own."
Laszlo Bock, Senior Vice President of People Operations, Google

ATOMIC HABITS

by James Clear

This book has a five star rating from 4,300 reviews. That's impressive. Everyone has at least a few bad habits, but beginning your financial journey might require losing behaviours you didn't previously consider to be bad. The structure of this book will help you. It won't be a free ride – you'll need to make some effort. Here's the blurb:

People think when you want to change your life, you need to think big. But world-renowned habits expert James Clear has discovered another way. He knows that real change comes from the compound effect of hundreds of small decisions: doing two push-ups a day, waking up five minutes early, or holding a single short phone call. He calls them atomic habits. In this ground-breaking book, Clear reveals exactly how these minuscule changes can grow into such life-altering outcomes. He uncovers a handful of simple life hacks, and delves into cutting-edge psychology and neuroscience to explain why they matter. Along the way, he tells inspiring stories of Olympic gold medallists, leading CEOs, and distinguished scientists who have used the science of tiny habits to stay productive, motivated, and happy. These small changes will have a revolutionary effect on your career, your relationships, and your life.

MONEY

by Laura Whateley

Written primarily for 20+ young adults clueless about finance, it is still relevant to Millennials. The ideas are clearly presented with plenty of humour. I highly recommend it.

What I particularly liked about this book is Laura's ability to address the needs of her target market. The book talks about the practical problems of flat sharing and the financial issues that arise and how to handle them. Laura is an award-winning journalist and The Times newspaper consumer champion.

SIDE HUSTLE AND 100 SIDE HUSTLES

by Chris Guillebeau

If increasing your income while keeping your day job appeals to you, then Chris' book entitled Side Hustle will help you develop and implement a plan. I haven't read it myself, but it has garnered 4½ stars out of 5 from 354 ratings. If you're looking for side hustle ideas, try 100 Side Hustles (4½ from 103 reviews). This book gives case studies on how people developed and ran specific side businesses (sometimes quite weird and wonderful), which, in many instances, turn into new careers.

One of the best blogs on starting your own side business, or indeed any business, is Smart Passive Income (**bit.ly/3ljMYLM**). Targeted at entrepreneurs, you'll find plenty of tools, podcasts, courses and articles here.

For more ideas and information on side hustles search YouTube and Podcasts.

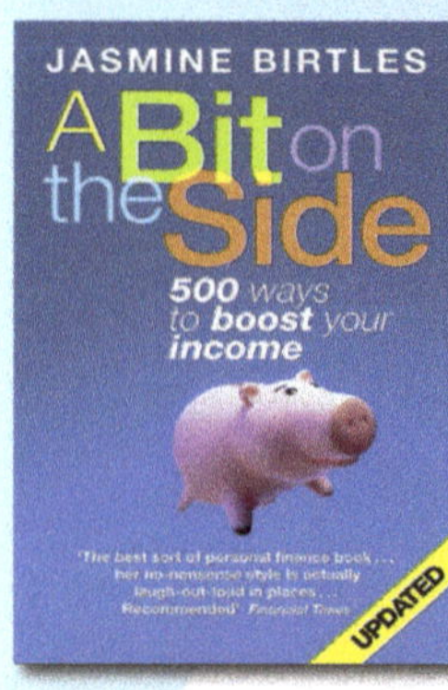

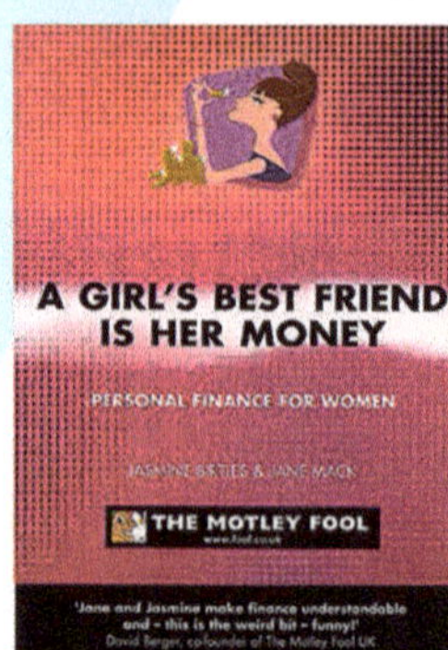

These books by Jasmine Birtles look interesting

Glossary **of investment terms (bit.ly/3sCRxUO)**

RECOMMENDED BLOGS & VLOGS

There are a huge number of money related blogs, but here are a few of my favourites to help you at this stage of your financial journey…

MoneySavingExpert
Cutting your costs, fighting your corner

The daddy of them all, MoneySavingExpert by Martin Lewis, is outstanding. Martin is an exceptional communicator and passionate about helping people on their financial journeys. MoneySavingExpert (MSE) is a phenomenal resource for just about anything. If you can't see a topic you're interested in, just use the search feature (the archives are an absolute treasure trove).

Recently MSE has joined forces with The Open University to provide a FREE and short course (12 hours over 6 modules), entitled Academy of Money (**bit.ly/3sLLzSu**). I haven't studied it myself, but with two such august institutions involved my guess is it will be of immeasurable quality and lasting value. At the end of the course you will be better able to:

- Budget effectively and know how to make good spending decisions.
- Grasp how income is taxed.
- Make sense of how and when to borrow money responsibly.
- Understand savings and investment products – including their different risks.
- Plan for retirement and know what to do if a projected pension is insufficient.

ThisisMoney.co.uk is another of my favourite websites/blogs. It's short articles on specific finance issues are clearly written with relevant and informative graphics. If I'm researching a topic I will always check-out what ThisisMoney has to say on the subject. Very highly recommended.

Money to the Masses and Be Clever with Your Cash are right up there too. Both blogs cover an extensive list of financial issues: from which are today's best consumer deals to what apps to use for your saving and investment journey. Both websites produce a weekly newsletter to which you might consider subscribing, they are filled with 'why didn't I think of that' or 'I never knew that' moments. Excellent.

Finally in this section, Holly MacKay's website Boring Money is a cracker. It's catchphrase is 'Free Money Advice for Normal People,' and it does what it says on the tin! It offers links to helpful websites (look under the Financial Advice tab and select Free Tips & Help), it additionally includes detailed answers by qualified investment advisers to many questions.

If you have a specific question, which you think is unique or unusual, chances are you'll find it on Boring Money (select Common Questions tab). Unfortunately the website forces you to scroll through 40+ pages to review all the questions – but it's worth it. Here you will find answers to questions you never thought you needed. Pure gold!

Boring Money's unique strength is guiding you to select the best investment platform for your specific needs. I review this website in much greater detail in MYFE Book 3.

The more you learn, the more you'll earn.

Warren Buffett

OTHER QUALITY BLOGS

Wannabefree **by Grainne McNamee**, author of How to Get Out of Debt, is an interesting and potentially helpful blog.

As an alternative to Meaningful Academy, you might want to try the Conversation of Money online training course. I haven't watched this series of planning and investing videos, but the outline looks interesting, and at £99.99 is great value.

Peter Komolafe is the presenter of a YouTube channel and offers many free videos, podcasts and blogs, including his views on various money saving and investing apps. I recommend them. What Peter has to say is both insightful and wise. Finally, Peter also offers one-on-one mentoring, coaching and a financial planning review service. The cost is £150 for 1½ hours, which is a good deal. My sense is you'll find it informative, constructive and worthwhile.

TheMoneyPrinciple is an engaging, helpful and compassionate website/blog by Maria, a business school professor. It is divided into four 'pillars': Make Money, Control Spending, Get Out of Debt, Invest for the Future. There are also some useful tools available here (**bit.ly/2YooXJY**), the compound calculator (**bit.ly/3qWzdWa**) is especially good. I like the way Maria kicks-off a conversation on her blog and allows people to post comments which are often very informative.

Making Money Simple is a promising new website/blog by Ryan aimed at those, like himself, new to investing. I particularly liked Ryan's uTube video on How to start investing in 2021 & My Vanguard Portfolio (**bit.ly/39ZIVRW**). The presentation is delivered jargon-free and Ryan uses informative screenshots of his own funds to illustrate how the Vanguard platform works and the information it gives you. In addition there is a freely available e-book Making Investing Simple available here (**bit.ly/2LMAVdK**). A great start with some exciting future vlogs promised.

Jason Butler is a Chartered Fellow of both the Chartered Institute for Securities & Investment and the Personal Finance Society and the author of this website/blog. Jason produces many helpful articles, books and tools of value to everyone under the general categories of Building Wealth, Money Conversations, Money Habits and Money Mindset. Articles range from Is Money Causing Conflict with Your Partner, through Money Myths Debunked to Are You On Course With Your Money? A highly useful and recommended resource.

Here's a list of three specialist blogs:

The Money Fox **by Francesca**, offers useful advice, especially for working mums.

Much More With Less **by Faith**, achieves exactly that.

Mr Money Moustache is a leading and exciting blogger on achieving early financial independence (FIRE).

Glossary **of investment terms (bit.ly/3sCRxUO)**

IF YOU'RE IN A HURRY

If you like watching free short videos, I recommend visiting:

bogleheads (**bit.ly/3cg9t11**). This is a website supported by fans of John Bogle, the creator of index funds, aka trackers, and Vanguard, the world's second largest fund management company. These short videos offer a quick overview of how to begin your savings and investment journey. Even if you're not ready to invest yet, watching these videos is an education in itself and will familiarise you with the terminology and possible investment options you will face.

An alternative high quality video guide is available at:

The Evidenced-Based Investor (**bit.ly/3sLcKgl**). There are many videos on this website covering numerous excellent topics. It's an extensive library.

SOME HELPFUL LINKS

The Wise Monkey has a really extensive and thoughtfully compiled list of links. I recommend you check it out here (**bit.ly/3n1eWOH**).

The DebtCamel is a highly regarded UK website for those with debt issues.

ONLINE FINANCIAL CALCULATORS

Online financial calculators are an invaluable shortcut to understanding numerous scenarios. Three of the best resources can be found at Candid Money (**bit.ly/30mqLom**), This is Money (**bit.ly/34f7YfW**), Monevator (**bit.ly/3n9WtPy**). Monevator also has some other suggestions here (**bit.ly/2GrbKut**). It all depends on what you're trying to establish and which calculator you find most intuitive.

Online calculators can produce slightly different outputs despite entering the same variables. This is rarely a problem. The discrepancies arise due to the slight mathematical deviations in the calculator's programming. For example, even rounding and the number of decimal places used under the bonnet can make small numbers compounded over many years appear different. However, these variances tend to be small, and in the general scheme of things are not significant.

I would like to make one essential addition to this list: The Financial Conduct Authority (FCA) (bit.ly/3cAuUdi). This is the landing page enabling you to check if an individual or firm is FCA authorised – an absolutely vital step before you discuss your financial affairs or give your money to anyone. Furthermore, as the recent London & Capital Finance fiasco illustrated, it isn't enough to validate the regulatory credentials of the individual and their company, you must also be sure the products/services being sold to you are likewise FCA regulated. Just as critically, be sure to avoid criminally cloned websites by checking The FCA Warning List. Just because a firm's registration number matches their FCA registration number doesn't mean you've landed on the correct webpage!

AND PLEASE DON'T FORGET

If you've enjoyed and benefited from this book, please consider making a donation to my chosen charity below.

THE BRAIN TUMOUR CHARITY

Please donate at JustGiving (bit.ly/3xelewo)

THANK YOU

Writing a book such as this has only been possible because I have been allowed to stand on the shoulders of giants: the many authors who have shared their professional investment knowledge. They are too numerous to name, but it is fundamentally their expertise and wisdom I share with you through these books.

In addition, no writer is able to complete their task without the support and generosity of others. I'm particularly indebted to the following:

William J. Bernstein whose short essays have informed the structure of these books. **Ian Millward** of Candid Financial Advice who, having read my first draft, diplomatically and constructively helped me to 'up' my game. **Justin Modray**, also of Candid, who kindly verified some tricky investment equations. Additionally, **Adam Gerrard** of Candid, who patiently answered my many questions. An old and valued friend and professional investor, **Brian Price** read my various revised chapters and gave his extensive wisdom clearly and willingly. **Warren Taylor** of WT Tax generously reviewed, and succinctly guided me through some of the thorny tax issues while simultaneously adding to my education. **Alison Quick** of Refinitiv Datastream, whose ability and speed at extracting historical investment market datasets is something to behold, and who always responded to my requests with patience and humour, as well as making invaluable suggestions. **Simon Harrington**, a pension specialist, who kindly walked me through some of the knotty pension assumptions. **Benjamin Lloyd** of benjaminlloyd.com, whose tenacity, skills and alacrity at research, maths and graphing software are impressive and without whom I would have struggled. **Danny Bowles** of Topper Consultancy, my editor, whose focus and insight, together with his candour, made my writing more accessible. **Matt Dettmar**, the UK's Leonardo da Vinci of magazine design (magazinedesigner.co.uk), whose creativity turned a dry subject into this more engaging book. **Clay**, my friend and neighbour (an award-winning writer himself), who always smiled when being given yet another draft to proof. Clay's insightful and straightforward feedback was a lesson in itself. I have also been blessed with many beta readers whose arms I've twisted to read my various manuscripts, especially **Dafydd**, **Claire**, **Richard**, **Saul**, **Robin**, **Susan**, **Steve** and **Johnny**, who made important observations that influenced the content and style. Thank you all.

Notwithstanding the knowledge and kindness of the above-mentioned individuals, any and all mistakes in MYFE are mine alone. Nevertheless, I could not have even begun my writing journey without the help and guidance of these generous people.

Finally, my deepest thanks go to my wife. Living with a first-time author is no easy gig. As writers we bounce between moments of elation and desperation; we stare into oblivion absorbed with re-writing a sentence; we disappear to our desks for days on end, and after all that, we're still never truly satisfied. My wife's humour, constant encouragement and her willingness to spend chunks of our savings to get this project off the ground made my writing experience all the more fun, exciting and memorable. Couldn't have done it without you, **A**.

ABOUT THE AUTHOR

Mark is a retired businessman, married with three children and three grandchildren.

Born and schooled in the UK, Mark grew up in England, West Africa, East Africa and France. After graduating with a business studies degree he spent four years living and working in the Far East followed by ten years in the USA. Mark and his family moved back to the UK in the early 1990s where he and his wife now live.

Given Mark's lack of formal financial qualifications, you might wonder why he thinks the MYFE series of books may be of value to you. The answer is, perhaps like you, he approached the saving and investment markets innocently and naïvely. Big mistake. And yet, this initial lack of knowledge about financial matters is one reason why Mark can now ask key questions to which many of us need straight answers – and too rarely get!

In short, Mark hopes a book written by someone like you, and for you, will be of empathetic and unique value.

The information in this series of MYFE books is based on Mark's own experiences, research and opinion. He receives nothing for writing these books. All costs, including research, data sourcing, fact checking, editing, legal overview, design, production, website development/hosting and marketing are absorbed by Mark.

So, why did Mark write these books?

1. To help his kids and others who could use free, sympathetic and unbiased financial guidance.
2. To spread the knowledge.
3. To raise money for his favoured charity.

It was also a pleasure for Mark to be able to create a special dyslexic edition.

JUST SO YOU KNOW...

Please don't assume that simply because these books are free there must be another, and ulterior, motive for writing them. This is not a business. These books are not loss-leaders for some other activity. There is nothing in this website that gives Mark any income, and he doesn't make money by referring you to other websites through the embedded hyperlinks. As such, when you visit MYFE.guide you will discover no advertising is accepted. You will not be spammed and you will not receive promotions from third-parties. Your name, or digital footprint, will never be sold to anyone or any company.

www.ingramcontent.com/pod-product-compliance
Lightning Source LLC
LaVergne TN
LVHW071201210926
848482LV00014B/705